FOUNDATIONS UNDER FIRE

FOUNDATIONS UNDER FIRE

Edited by
THOMAS C. REEVES

Cornell University Press

ITHACA AND LONDON

To Frank Kelly

Preface

A BROAD and reasonably objective look at America's private tax-exempt foundations has been needed for quite some time. The information available about these numerous, often wealthy, frequently controversial organizations is sparse, and the presentation is usually polemical. For a variety of reasons, foundations have not been willing to open their records to historians. In preparing my history of the Fund for the Republic, I was well aware how fortunate I had been in obtaining complete access to a foundation's files. Since a comprehensive study of foundations is thus nearly out of the question, owing to the lack of available source materials, a collection of readings about foundations and their critics would seem to be especially useful.

This book attempts to provide a balanced and provocative set of readings about this subject of national concern. I have made no attempt to cover the technicalities of the tax structure, for the dialogue the book is intended to stimulate and assist may be most effectively carried on by those other than attorneys and accountants. Nor did I choose to examine any but the major topics that have concerned critics. Arguments over such matters as the wisdom of making grants to individuals as opposed to groups, though sometimes fruitful, are not included here.

Special thanks go to Professor Eugene Halaas of the University of Denver, an economist of great wisdom. I am also indebted to the staff of Cornell University Press for their encouragement.

T. R.

Colorado Springs
March 1970

Acknowledgments

I wish to acknowledge permission granted to reprint the following material (complete publishing information is given on the first page of each excerpt):

Excerpt from the editorial, "Taxing the Foundations," reprinted by permission from *The Christian Science Monitor*, © 1969, The Christian Science Publishing Society; all rights reserved.

Excerpts from René A. Wormser, *Foundations: Their Power and Influence*, published by Devin-Adair Co., copyright 1958 by René A. Wormser.

Excerpts from the following articles in *Foundation News*: F. Emerson Andrews, "Foundation Funds—Whose Money?" and "Views of The Treasury Report"; Mortimer M. Caplin, "Foundations and the Government: Some Observations on the Future"; Burton Raffel, "A Critique of American Foundations"; and Donald Young, "Support for Social Research"; copyright 1963, 1968, 1963, 1965, and 1963 by the Foundation Center.

Excerpt from John W. Gardner, "A Whip That Could Cripple Many Public Services," Washington *Post*, June 8, 1969.

Excerpts from *Wealth and Culture* by Eduard C. Lindeman; copyright, 1936, by Harcourt, Brace & World, Inc.; renewed, 1964, by Eduard C. Lindeman; reprinted by permission of the publishers.

Excerpt from *Corporation Giving in a Free Society* by Richard Eells, copyright © 1956 by Harper & Row, Publishers, Incorporated.

Excerpt from *U.S. Philanthropic Foundations: Their History, Structure, Management, and Record* by Warren Weaver; copyright © 1967 by the American Academy of Arts & Sciences.

Excerpt from Robert M. Hutchins, *Freedom, Education, and the Fund: Essays and Addresses, 1946–1956,* published by Meridian, 1956.

Excerpts from *The Nation:* Fred J. Cook, "Charity Begins at Home: Foundations as a Tax Dodge," April 20, 1963, and Robert G. Sherrill, "Foundation Pipe Lines: The Beneficent CIA," May 9, 1966; by permission of the publisher.

Excerpt from the syndicated column "To Be Equal" by Whitney M. Young, Jr., in the Colorado Springs *Free Press,* July 20, 1969; by permission of the National Urban League, Inc.

Kenneth Crawford, "The Rooney Reform," *Newsweek,* March 3, 1969; copyright Newsweek, Inc., March, 1969.

Excerpt from Alan Pifer, "The Report of the President," in the *Annual Report for the Fiscal Year Ended September 30, 1968,* the Carnegie Corporation; by permission.

Excerpt from Wright Patman, "The Free-Wheeling Foundations," *The Progressive,* June, 1967; by permission.

Excerpt from *Danger on the Right* by Arnold Forster and Benjamin R. Epstein; copyright © 1964 by Anti-Defamation League of B'nai B'rith; reprinted by permission of Random House, Inc.

Excerpt from Albert M. Sacks, "The Role of Philanthropy: An Institutional View," *Virginia Law Review,* April, 1960; by permission of Fred B. Rothman & Co.

Contents

CONTENTS

FOUNDATIONS
UNDER FIRE

Introduction

AMERICANS have long been known for their generosity, and in recent years philanthropy has enjoyed an unprecedented boom. In 1967 alone Americans gave away some fifteen billion dollars—about forty million dollars a day.

Hundreds of thousands of American charitable organizations have been granted tax-exempt status. Private tax-exempt foundations grew greatly in number and financial strength during the affluent 1960's. By late 1969 there were more than 22,000, with new ones being created at an unprecedented and increasingly rapid rate. One congressional study revealed that by the end of 1967 the assets of 647 foundations under review had increased almost 75 per cent in seven years. Two years later total foundation assets were estimated to be in excess of twenty billion dollars. Although these assets pale when compared to total government spending or to the gross national product, foundations control the nation's largest pool of independent funds. In 1968 foundations made grants totaling approximately 1.5 billion dollars. And the impact of foundations is often even greater than their assets and allocations suggest. As one observer noted recently, "It is now impossible to conceive of contemporary enterprise in education, research and international development without simultaneously thinking of Carnegie, Rockefeller and Ford."[1]

[1] Peter Schragg, review of Warren Weaver *et al.*, *U.S. Philan-*

But for all of their wealth and influence, foundations have become acutely sensitive in recent years to attacks from a wide variety of critics. As one foundation staff report put it, "A recurring uneasiness pervades the foundation field." [2] Another wrote of "storm warnings of trouble" looming ahead "for foundations and all of philanthropy, as represented by the tax-exempt privilege." [3] An appraisal published in 1967 by a distinguished foundation executive posed as its central question: "Does the positive record of the American philanthropic foundations justify the continuing existence of these tax-free institutions?" [4] The President of the Carnegie Corporation warned late in 1968 that foundations had to put their "house in better order" or risk "hasty and clumsy" regulative legislation from Congress.[5]

In 1956 Dwight Macdonald had written, "Almost the only way a foundation can subject itself to valid criticism is to pay for it." [6] While even then this statement was an exaggeration, events in subsequent years made it completely invalid. As never before, writers, scholars, and politicians were pointing an incriminating finger at tax-exempt foundations during the "taxpayers' revolt," which gathered momentum during the last year of the Johnson administration. A long-standing congressional probe contributed to the initiation of a sweeping re-

---

thropic Foundations: Their History, Structure, Management, and Record (New York: Harper and Row, 1967), in New York *Times* Book Review, October 22, 1967, p. 3.

[2] "Foundations: An Overview," *Foundation News,* 8 (November, 1967), 117.

[3] "1967 Review," *Foundation News,* 9 (January, 1968), 5.

[4] Weaver *et al., U.S. Philanthropic Foundations,* p. xv.

[5] "Foundations Warned to Put 'House in Better Order,' " Colorado Springs *Free Press,* December 15, 1968.

[6] *The Ford Foundation: The Men and the Millions* (New York: Reynal, 1956), p. 125.

view of the federal tax code. Tens of thousands of Americans were reading such books as *The Money Game, The Rich: Are They Different?*, and *The Rich and the Super-Rich*, which publicized the financial manipulations of foundations by their donors. Presidential candidate George Wallace told his millions of followers that foundations should no longer receive favored treatment, and he pledged to "require these organizations to assume their rightful responsibility as to the operation of our Government." [7] University faculty members and students were outraged by evidence of collusion between foundations and the Central Intelligence Agency. Some foundations were linked with political extremism, college rioting, political campaigning, and a prolonged New York public school strike. A few observers questioned the continued existence of foundations in an era of expanding governmental involvement in areas of American life, such as medical and scientific research and help for the poor, that had traditionally been the responsibility of private philanthropy.

Foundations are private instruments through which tax-exempt funds are channeled toward public purposes. As aptly defined by F. Emerson Andrews, the foundation is "a non-governmental, non-profit organization having a principal fund of its own, managed by its own trustees or directors, and established to maintain or aid social, educational, charitable, religious, or other activities serving the common welfare. Both charitable trusts and corporations are included." [8] This generally accepted definition distinguishes foundations from thou-

[7] "Excerpts from American Independent Platform," New York *Times*, October 14, 1968.

[8] Introduction to Ann D. Walton and Marianna O. Lewis, eds., *The Foundation Directory*, Edition 2 (New York: Russell Sage Foundation, 1964), p. 9.

3

sands of fund-raising groups, organizations, and corporations —such as the Red Cross, churches, and colleges—which in 1968 expended about 91 per cent of the total charitable and philanthropic funds in the United States.

The foundations that fit into Andrews' definition fall into five classifications:

1. General-purpose foundations
2. Special-purpose foundations
3. Family or personal foundations
4. Corporation (or company-sponsored) foundations
5. Community foundations.

The general-purpose category includes almost all of the large, well-known organizations, such as the Carnegie Corporation of New York, the Duke Endowment, and the Ford and Rockefeller foundations. They usually possess substantial assets (Ford alone has more than three billion dollars), are governed by a board of trustees or directors, employ a professional staff, and offer a broad, flexible program.

The special-purpose foundations disburse funds within specific areas, such as education, medicine, archaeology, or the advancement of peace. The Edward Drummond Libbey Trust, for example, pays the net income from its multi-million-dollar endowment exclusively to the Toledo, Ohio, Museum of Art.

Family or personal foundations are the most numerous. They normally serve to channel the founder's current giving, and have no professional staff, trustees, or directors. Their assets are usually small and are managed by a single accountant or attorney in close association with the donor or his family. The Ford Foundation began as a family foundation, moving to the general-purpose category at Henry Ford's death.

The corporation foundation is a relatively new and fast-growing development. While it is legally separate from the parent company, its trustees, directors, and officers are recruited mainly from company ranks. It administers current giving usually aimed at advancing the welfare of the parent corporation, its employees, or stockholders. The Bulova Watch Company Foundation, for example, furnished free training to disabled war veterans as watch repairmen.

Community foundations serve to manage local charitable gifts made in perpetuity. They are controlled by boards of community leaders and are usually created for specific purposes. Among community foundations are the Chicago Community Trust, and the Buffalo, Cleveland, Indianapolis, and Minneapolis foundations.

Foundations are largely a phenomenon of twentieth-century America. Charitable contributions were allowed as deductions in 1917, four years after the implementation of the Sixteenth Amendment. In 1936 Congress passed a law permitting business firms to deduct 5 per cent of their net income before taxes for charity. In 1964 a revision in the tax structure allowed up to 20 per cent of an individual's gross adjusted income to be exempt from income tax. Income from foundation investments (with certain restrictions) and gifts and bequests donated to foundations are also tax-free. Thus, Congress has consistently been willing to encourage private philanthropy by offering tax relief to donors.

Foundations have been created and supported, of course, for the highest, most idealistic reasons, among them the genuine desire to help others and the wish to distribute funds for the public welfare in an intelligent and systematic way. The billions of dollars spent by foundations in the United States and around the world have achieved highly impressive results, as many books, articles, and reports sponsored or encouraged by foundations themselves will attest. The public relations efforts of foundations dominate foundation literature. But beyond the idealism and the much-deserved praise lies the less-publicized fact of the economic advantages enjoyed by foundations, advantages that bring with them a host of attendant issues and challenges.

The primary impetus for the proliferation of foundations seems certainly to have been federal tax laws. Through foundations wealthy individuals and corporations have been able legally to reduce and circumvent taxes, often saving themselves large sums of money. (The Treasury Department reported that, in 1968, no income taxes were paid by 155 persons earning over $200,000—including 21 who earned at least one million dollars. John D. Rockefeller III, for example, was able to avoid them altogether because of his large charitable donations.) And foundations often permit retention of control of wealth, a benefit unavailable with donations to operating charities such as the Heart Fund.

The rise of the corporation foundation may be directly related to the excess-profits taxes of the Korean War years. The high personal income taxes of the Second World War caused a leap in the number of family foundations. The Ford family employed a foundation at Henry Ford's death to maintain control of a gigantic business corporation and to save an estimated 321 million dollars in inheritance taxes. In short, the higher federal taxes of the past few decades have undoubtedly advanced the unprecedented growth of foundations.

In 1967 more than half of the 236 foundations with assets over ten million dollars had been created since 1940. Half of the 1,210 foundations holding assets between one million and ten million dollars had begun operation since 1950. In the summer of 1967 the *Wall Street Journal* described the operations of a tax consulting firm that specialized in creating philanthropic foundations and trusts, and that charged a fee of $10,500 per customer. A company spokesman claimed that the firm had served more than eight hundred clients in a little over a year—if true, accounting for more than one-half of the new foundations estimated to have come into existence in that period.

Charges against foundations often revolve around the fundamental issue of "public responsibility," i.e., the degree of control that the public should have over the private expenditure of tax-free dollars. How responsible should foundations be to the taxpayer? To what degree may the public define the "public purposes" of foundations?

Critics have frequently claimed that tax concessions and incentives are merely "loopholes," devices beyond the reach of the average citizen whereby the rich abscond with dollars normally destined for the Treasury Department.[9] The Reece Committee (see the Reece Report on Tax-Exempt Foundations) took the position that tax-free dollars were public dollars, to be spent in ways acceptable to current public opinion. More than one foundation polemicist, on the other hand, has denied that philanthropic institutions owe any responsibility to the public, arguing that untaxed money remains privately owned. Foundation spokesmen have often completely evaded the issue of public responsibility or have woven careful language around it. "No one has any right to object to the tax-free dollars available to philanthropy until he has made a reasonable effort to learn what these dollars accomplish."[10]

The precise nature of funds utilized by foundations has

[9] See "Taxes and Philanthropy Survey," *Foundation News*, 8 (September, 1967), 87–88.
[10] Weaver *et al.*, *U.S. Philanthropic Foundations*, pp. 88–89.

never been determined. The state and federal status supervising the tax status of foundations have spelled out little more than broad principles of policy, and the perimeters of governmental responsibility for the operations of foundations have been consistently vague. This is not surprising, since foundations are tied to many of the nation's most powerful individuals and corporations, traditionally averse to the expansion of government regulation.

The consensus of recent years among officials of the Internal Revenue Service (the organization on the federal level most directly involved in foundation activities) and "philanthropoids" (professional foundation officers employed by the larger foundations) seems to be that foundations do owe a minimum accountability to the public, that the obligation should be met voluntarily, and that it should take the form of published annual or semi-annual reports the contents of which should be left to the discretion of the foundations. This view is put forward, from varying perspectives, by Richard Eells, F. Emerson Andrews, and Alan Pifer in the selections that follow.

With few exceptions, foundations have traditionally shrouded their affairs in secrecy, claiming that their business was exclusively their own. When Eduard C. Lindeman started out in the late 1920's to write a book on foundations, he discovered to his surprise that "those who managed foundations and trusts did not wish to have these instruments investigated. Had it occurred to me then that it would require eight years of persistent inquiry at a wholly disproportionate cost to disclose even the basic quantitative facts desired, I am sure that the study would have been promptly abandoned." [11]

[11] *Wealth and Culture* (New York: Harcourt, Brace, 1936), p. vii.

When Frederick P. Keppel, head of the Carnegie Corporation, wrote his book *The Foundation* in 1930 he was disturbed: "I myself, who am professionally interested in such matters and ought to be in a position to secure available information, have been able to obtain nothing whatever regarding three foundations, the announced capitalization of which aggregates seventy-five million dollars." [12]

When Harold C. Coffman was conducting research for *American Foundations: A Study of Their Role in the Child Welfare Movement*, published in 1936, he was forced to supplement the few annual reports at his disposal with 231 recorded interviews and correspondence amounting to over 1,-000 letters. He complained, "Many foundations feel that their activities are private, and that they do not have a responsibility of reporting them to the public." [13]

In 1956, when F. Emerson Andrews published his *Philanthropic Foundations,* he knew of only 107 foundations that issued reports. By 1965, J. Richard Taft, editor of *Foundation News,* could count only 212 foundations that published reports, 116 of which "could be classified as regular reporters." [14] While many of the largest general-purpose foundations published reviews of their activities and assets, Taft said, only one of the sixteen company-sponsored foundations with assets over ten million dollars issued reports, and not a single one of the ten largest family foundations. Fifteen foundations, all with assets over fifty million dollars, were releasing no reports in 1965.

Two Congressional investigations in the early 1950's occa-

[12] *The Foundation: Its Place in American Life* (New York: Macmillan, 1930), p. 56.

[13] (New York: Association Press, 1936), p. 7.

[14] J. Richard Taft, "Reporting: Problems and Realities," *Foundation News,* 6 (September, 1965), 89.

sioned much alarm among the larger foundations, and to avoid further criticism channels were established to provide the public with a modicum of information. In 1956 the Foundation Library Center (now the Foundation Center) was created to accumulate and disseminate data. Its bimonthly journal, *Foundation News*, was first published in 1960, and was later supplemented with a *Bulletin* and a series of "Occasional Papers." These publications, along with those of the Council on Foundations, another private clearinghouse, quickly became the most readily available and comprehensive (although frequently biased) sources of information on foundations.

The Revenue Act of 1950 first permitted public inspection of annual forms filed by foundations with the Internal Revenue Service. But the forms revealed little, and many foundations failed to submit them. By 1962 several changes had been made in the forms, and more facts were available to the public, including officers' salaries, investment holdings, accumulation of capital gains and other income, relationships with contributors, names and addresses of donees, and amounts and types of grants. Additional information, such as the names of donors and facts surrounding unrelated business income of more than $1,000, was collected but was not available for public inspection. Many foundations only partially completed the new forms and others failed to file them. There was little or no reaction from the Internal Revenue Service.

While sources of information have improved in recent years, much remains unknown about the thousands of foundations operating within the United States. After several years of prodding by Congressman Wright Patman's Subcommittee on Foundations, the Internal Revenue Service late in 1968 prepared a list containing the names and addresses of 30,262 foundations—the first time the federal government had ever attempted to total the number of foundations in the country. When subcommittee staff members wrote to the first several thousand foundations on the list, around 1,000 letters were returned for having improper addresses. They discovered that several of the foundations listed had been out of existence for years (one for a decade) and that many duplications and other errors were to be found in the government's compilation. Congressman Patman said, "If the Internal Revenue Service cannot even come up with the current addresses of the organizations for which they have responsibility, I shudder to think of the kind of audit and review that is being undertaken by them." [15]

In 1969 both the House of Representatives and the Senate Finance Committee favored a requirement that foundations file more complete and up-to-date information with the federal government. Many questions remain, however, after the most complete statistics are filled in on a federal information return: the soundness of operating principles, the qualifications of trustees and staff members, the rate and quality of achievement in relation to the amount of expenditure, to name a few.

James A. Perkins, former Vice President of the Carnegie Corporation, wrote in 1963, "A foundation has to work between two very powerful imperatives—freedom in the public interest, and public supervision in the public interest." [16] The adequacy of self-constructed reports and tax forms as the full measure of public accountability is an open question, worthy of much closer scrutiny.

[15] U.S., Congress, House, Statement by Representative Wright Patman before the Senate Finance Committee, 91st Cong., 1st Sess., October 9, 1969, *Congressional Record*, p. H9389.

[16] "What the New Foundation Executive Should Know," *Foundation News*, 4 (September, 1963), 1.

The most common foundation argument against a federal law requiring increased public information is that accountability leads to control. The leading contention for the value of foundations, at least since the First World War, has been that they may do what government and the thousands of fundraising charities cannot or should not do. "Foundation executives and their trustees are well aware," the President of the Research Corporation wrote in 1962, "that the venturesome and the unorthodox are the essence of the reason for the foundations' establishment and for their continuing existence in the framework of our society." [17]

Foundations can, it is claimed, be far more daring, flexible, and expeditious than government. (One philanthropoid emphasized recently that in the Rockefeller Foundation grants up to $20,000 may be made within 24 hours and require the signatures of only three officers.) Foundations are equipped to attempt the experimental, to expand the frontiers of knowledge, to go where bureaucracy, public opinion, and politics forbid government intervention. As a Treasury Department report of 1965 states: "Private philanthropy plays a special and vital role in our society. . . . Private philanthropic organizations can be uniquely qualified to initiate thought and action, experiment with new and untried ventures, dissent from prevailing attitudes, and act quickly and flexibly." [18] This is the concept of "venture" or "risk capital," and at a time of rapid federal involvement in an ever broader spectrum of human concerns, it is critical to the continued prosperity —perhaps even existence—of foundations.

[17] See [J. William Hinkley], "The Effects of Public Accountability," *Foundation News*, 5 (May, 1964), 9.

[18] *Treasury Department Report on Private Foundations*, Committee on Finance, United States Senate, 89th Cong., 1st Sess. (Washington, D.C.: U.S. Government Printing Office, 1965), p. 5.

The major, most opulent, and most influential foundations are controlled by boards of trustees and directors. The extent to which the often wealthy and distinguished citizens who serve on these boards might vote to support venturesome and unorthodox projects has long been questioned by critics. Surveys of foundation trustees in the 1930's by Harold C. Coffman and Eduard C. Lindeman revealed the great majority to be white, middle-aged, upper-middle-class, Protestant, Eastern lawyers, bankers, and businessmen, educated in private colleges and universities. In 1956, F. Emerson Andrews drew "a composite portrait" of trustees serving twenty large foundations: his findings were virtually identical with those of the earlier studies. When Philip M. Stern analyzed the credentials of the Ford Foundation's trustees in 1966, he contended that "with one probable exception there is not a non-Establishment man among the fifteen." In 1967, University of California sociologist G. William Domhoff published the results of a study showing that "twelve of the top 13 foundations are controlled by members of the power elite, with two-thirds of their trustees coming from the upper class (51 per cent) or major corporations (16 per cent)." [19]

The best gauge of venture capital would be the analysis of foundation achievements. What studies and records exist indicate clearly that foundations have been, for the most part, both cautious and traditional in their philanthropic giving. The historian Merle Curti wrote a few years ago:

Philanthropy on the whole has avoided controversial issues, the very issues, perhaps, that offer the greatest challenge and that point to the greatest need. . . . Urban renewal, the civil liberties,

[19] See Philip M. Stern, "An Open Letter to the Ford Foundation," *Harper's*, 232 (January, 1966), 85; G. William Domhoff, *Who Rules America* (New York: Prentice-Hall, 1967), p. 65.

racial injustice, overseas relief and technical aid, and international peace and understanding, have . . . attracted some philanthropic support. But, in terms of the importance and need, I venture to maintain that what has been done—in terms of the giving of money, time, and talent—has been utterly inadequate and far less worthy of the description of "venture capital" and social inventiveness than much of the literature of philanthropy suggests.[20]

One critic contended in 1968, "The influence of the rich in philanthropy focuses on the established institution, tends to maintain the *status quo*. It is rare, indeed, that major donations are made to encourage basic change or even minor dislocation of any aspect of established society." [21]

Philanthropoids themselves have often been critical of foundation timidity, as the selections by Donald Young and Burton Raffel reveal. They and others have pointed out that the billions of dollars held by these corporations and trusts could be put to work much more effectively in such complex areas as slum rebuilding, urban transportation, conservation, mental health, the mass media, the humanities, population control, civil liberties education, and international disarmament. Imagination and daring, critics have charged, appear to be the ingredients most noticeably lacking in the exercise of foundation philanthropy.

By the mid-1960's, however, there were signs that significant quantities of foundation dollars might at last be heading for increasingly controversial outlets. From 1964 to 1965 the amount channeled by the larger foundations into "interracial relations" jumped from 2.3 million dollars to 26.7

[20] "Creative Giving: Slogan or Reality?" *Foundation News*, 3 (November, 1962), 8–9.
[21] George G. Kirstein, "Philanthropy: The Golden Crowbar," *The Nation*, 207 (September 16, 1968), 239.

million dollars. At the nineteenth annual conference of the Council on Foundations, in May, 1968, urban problems and race relations were of major interest. One Urban League official expressed the belief that many foundations were beginning to reshape their thinking about civil rights. The *Foundation News* report of grants for 1968 revealed a substantial shift in the interest of foundations toward poverty-associated projects; a sum estimated at 270 million dollars was spent that year in this area.

Perhaps the most newsworthy item from the world of philanthropy in the past few years has been the growing concern of the Ford Foundation about social problems. Where this largest of foundations had once allowed its first president, Paul G. Hoffman, to resign, in part for his untraditional daring and courage, it now proclaimed through McGeorge Bundy (its president since mid-1966) that it would place an unlimited part of its investment portfolio in enterprises expected to bring a "high social yield." Announced investments included a loan of one million dollars for working capital for a South Carolina steel company, largely owned and operated by its Negro employees; the purchase of stock in a Philadelphia corporation in the business of building Negro shopping centers; and an investment in a trust company engaged in purchasing and integrating apartment houses in white neighborhoods. Bundy said that investments might range from family planning to cooperatives.

That same year ten other prominent foundations were awaiting a federal ruling permitting them to create a joint tax-exempt fund to make investments in "high risk" ghetto areas.

And yet critics might well question the adequacy and originality of such programs and proposals. To what extent have foundations followed the federal government into these fields? (David Halberstam noted recently that the Establishment discovered the race problem in the mid-1960's allegedly "when a commuter train to Manhattan from Greenwich was fired on by black youths as it waited at the 125th Street station.") [22] To what extent are foundation programs distinctive? To what degree do these programs reflect either foundation resources or the severity of the problems encountered? And what crusading experimentation has come from the thousands of family, corporation, and special-purpose foundations, rapidly multiplying—ostensibly for public purposes?

It is true, for example, that Ford allowed several small foundations to explore possibilities in civil rights before reluctantly lending a hand. Mitchell Sviridoff, head of the Ford Foundation's division of national affairs, states that he bets Ford's money on "the moderate middle"—meaning the solidly middle class Urban League and the N.A.A.C.P. Ford subsidiaries in this area, two Washington *Post* writers say, are "run by essentially the same class of people that run Ford," secure members of the Establishment like John Gardner, Carl Kaysen, and William Slayton, who may well be unable or unwilling to understand and fight the deepest-rooted, most severe problems of the ghetto.[23] Observable progress since 1965 in, say, Watts or Harlem, has been minimal at best. The squalid slums but a few blocks from the White House have successfully withstood the impact of "venture capital."

It may be that there are areas where "seed money" from the private sector initiates activities worthy of federal support.

[22] "The Very Expensive Education of McGeorge Bundy," *Harper's*, 239 (July, 1969), 37.

[23] Laurence Stern and Richard Harwood, "Ford Foundation: Its Works Spark a Backlash," Washington *Post*, November 2, 1969.

(The fund-raising charities, of course, are also in the private sector and spend far more money each year for charitable purposes than do foundations.) It may be, as McGeorge Bundy once contended, that foundations are needed as critics of government programs. It may even be that there are areas, such as the arts and the humanities, where government funds should be utilized sparingly to preserve independence. But if foundations are to display effectively their unique importance they may be required to document in detail their distinctive contributions to a world struggling desperately with the most disturbing questions ever faced by humanity. Peter Schragg wrote in 1967: "given the conditions of contemporary life, any foundation that operates by traditional wisdom will simply be irrelevant." [24]

Some philanthropoids have countered charges of timidity with the historical fact that Congress has investigated foundations four times, attacking them on each occasion for being involved in areas some legislators considered unpatriotic.

The first investigation took place during the Progressive Era and resulted in charges that foundations were tools of reaction dedicated to forwarding the cause of ultra-conservatism. The Walsh Committee hearings had little impact even at the time, and no legislation followed.

In 1934 Congress added to the requirements for income tax exemption, declaring that no substantial part of the activities of tax-exempt charitable and educational organizations could be used for carrying on propaganda or influencing legislation. The words "substantial," "propaganda," and "influence" required interpretation, of course, but for almost two decades

[24] Review of Weaver *et al.*, New York *Times* Book Review, October 22, 1967, p. 3.

foundations flourished virtually unaffected by these restrictions.

Then in the McCarthy era a committee of the House of Representatives under Eugene Cox of Georgia investigated foundations, "especially to determine which such foundations and organizations are using their resources for un-American and subversive activities or for purposes not in the interest or tradition of the United States." [25] Hearings were held in late 1952, featuring some forty witnesses, including officials of several large foundations.

The investigation was politically motivated (Cox had strong grievances against the Rockefellers, Fords, and Paul G. Hoffman, for supporting General Eisenhower against his own presidential candidate, Robert A. Taft) and took place in an election year. The fifteen-page final report, issued after Cox's untimely death, generally cleared foundations of charges that they had substantially assisted Communist and pro-Communist activities in the United States, adding that they "remain today an important and vital force in American life." [26] One of the committee members, however, was dissatisfied, and Representative Brazilla Carroll Reece of Tennessee soon acquired funds from Congress for a more "comprehensive" study of foundations.

In December, 1954, the Reece Committee published a 416-

[25] *Hearings before the Select Committee to Investigate Tax-Exempt Foundations and Comparable Organizations*, 82nd Cong., 2d Sess., (Washington, D.C.: U.S. Government Printing Office, 1953), p. 1.

[26] See *Final Report of the Select Committee to Investigate Foundations and Other Organizations*, U.S. House of Representatives, 82nd Cong., 2d Sess., Report No. 2514, (Washington, D.C.: U.S. Government Printing Office, 1953), p. 3.

page report which charged that a "diabolical conspiracy" existed between foundations and radical educational and research organizations, for the purpose of brainwashing the public with subversive ideologies. The report was a high point of the McCarthyite delirium, and is well represented by the selection from René Wormser, Committee Counsel.

The Reece Committee was ridiculed and scorned by an overwhelming majority of the nation's leading newspapers and magazines. And, once again, no legislation came out of the investigation. Dean Rusk, then president of the Rockefeller Foundation, commented in 1955:

I do not believe that foundations and their trustees have been intimidated by the events of the past two years. And I have no doubt but that ten or twenty years hence, whenever the next round of investigation comes, we shall have an interesting list of controversial items for consideration. Just which ones they shall be, we have no way of knowing, for that will depend upon the predilections of the investigator.[27]

There is little evidence that foundations were intimidated by the Cox and Reece committees, in spite of the latter's stern warning to trustees to be "very chary of promoting ideas, concepts and opinion-forming material which runs contrary to what the public currently wishes, approves and likes." Robert H. Bremner concluded accurately, "Whatever disservice the [Reece] Committee rendered the House, it did no serious harm to foundations."[28]

The next, and far more serious, probe of foundations was

[27] Quoted in F. Emerson Andrews, *Philanthropic Foundations* (New York: Russell Sage Foundation, 1956), p. 347.

[28] *American Philanthropy* (Chicago: University of Chicago Press, 1960), p. 176.

begun in 1961 by Congressman Wright Patman of Texas. This investigation was largely concerned with alleged financial malfeasance, but as early as his first report to the Select Committee On Small Business, issued late in 1962, Patman referred to the "subsidizing" of "antidemocratic propaganda." [29] His evidence soon pointed, rather, to foundation involvement with politics.

In 1964 Patman disclosed that the J. M. Kaplan Fund of New York had for five years served as "a conduit for channeling CIA funds," and went on to list a number of foundations that had contributed to the Fund. This led to evidence that CIA money had gone to a variety of groups, using foundations as "fronts." By 1967 scores of smaller foundations, including seven from Patman's home state, were linked to the CIA.[30]

In public hearings held in February, 1969, by the House Ways and Means Committee, Patman criticized Ford Foundation "study grants" to former aides of the late Senator Robert Kennedy. ("Were aides of Vice President Humphrey, Senator McCarthy, and Governor Wallace offered similar awards by the Ford Foundation?" he asked) and a grant to the Cleveland chapter of CORE, which supported a voter registration drive in the city's Negro ghetto. He also noted charges by Congressman John J. Rooney of New York that a political opponent had used foundation funds against him a year earlier in an attempt to defeat his bid for reelection. Asked Representative Patman: "Have the giant foundations made or do they

---

[29] *Tax-Exempt Foundations and Charitable Trusts: Their Impact on Our Economy-Chairman's Report to the Select Committee on Small Business*, U.S. House of Representatives, 87th Cong., (Washington, D.C.: U.S. Government Printing Office, 1962), p. 2.

[30] See "Funny Money," *The Nation*, 205 (December 4, 1967), 581.

plan to make grants that will aid certain candidates to run for national, state and local office?" [31]

Shortly afterward, Congressman Henry B. Gonzalez of Texas, a liberal Democrat, made headlines by condemning Ford Foundation support of the Mexican-American Youth Organization, a group run by young militants. (In this case, as in all similar cases, Ford severed its relations with those accused of political activism.)

Foundation involvement with members of the United States Supreme Court also made the front pages of newspapers in 1969, bringing shrill demands from certain members of Congress for greater restrictions on foundation activities. Justice Abe Fortas resigned from the Court when it was revealed that he had accepted a $20,000 fee from the family foundation of financier Louis E. Wolfson (Mr. Wolfson was in prison for violating a federal securities law). Justice William O. Douglas became the subject of controversy when it was learned that he was receiving a salary of $12,000 a year to serve as president of the Albert B. Parvin Foundation, which had large stock holdings in a firm owning three Las Vegas hotels and gambling casinos. Douglas resigned from the foundation "for health reasons" [32] and the American Bar Association's ethics committee refused to rule on the matter for lack of evidence.

Congressional critics were also encouraged by the Ford Foundation's abrasive encounter with the United Federation of Teachers in New York. As part of the Foundation's "new look" under the leadership of McGeorge Bundy, sizable grants were made to three New York school districts, located

[31] U.S., Congress, House, Statement by Representative Wright Patman before the House Committee on Ways and Means, 91st Cong., 1st Sess., February 18, 1969, *Congressional Record*, p. H1015.

[32] James R. Polk, "Douglas Ruling Rejected," Denver *Post*, May 24, 1969.

in Negro slum areas, to experiment with decentralization. Several teachers were subsequently dismissed by the local school board in the Ocean Hill–Brownsville district, and the teachers' union struck, demanding the virtual abolition of the entire experiment. The predominant issue was racial, and the Foundation became the vortex of the clash between poor blacks, Puerto Ricans, and the white establishment. Union president Albert Shanker said that the Foundation ought to be treated as a "political lobby," should lose its tax-exempt status, and should be subject to legislative investigation. In a lengthy reply, Bundy expressed the Foundation's and his personal support of decentralization but emphasized that funds had also been awarded to organizations headed by men who had been critical of decentralization. Moreover, Bundy said later, "if private foundations cannot assist experiments, their unique role will be impaired, to the detriment of American society. It would be tragic if the work of the great American foundations in such essential fields as population, educational reform and civil rights were stunted by irresponsible attacks." [33]

Charges were also made in the early and mid-1960's that foundations were subsidizing organizations of the Far Right. Investigation by the Internal Revenue Service led to the revocation of tax exemption for a few foundations, including one sponsored by the Texas billionaire H. L. Hunt.

In retrospect, it is difficult to believe that foundations, in particular the larger foundations, have as yet been inhibited

[33] See Robert M. Smith, "Shanker Says Ford Foundation Has Undue Influence in Schools," New York *Times*, November 11, 1968; Richard Reeves, "Bundy Condemns Influence Charges by Shanker," *ibid.*, November 13; Naomi Levine with Richard Cohen, *Ocean Hill–Brownsville, Schools in Crisis: A Case History* (New York: Popular Library, 1969), esp. the Afterword by the Ford Foundation's Mario Fantini, pp. 137–155.

by allegations of "un-American" activities, by charges of political partisanship, or by sanctions imposed against a handful of foundations employing blatant propaganda. Few foundation officials have ever contended that their use of "venture capital" was affected directly by the criticism. (As in the case of the New York teachers' strike, for example, the clamor neither adversely affected the Ford Foundation nor prevented the reelection of New York City's mayor.)

It is a fact that interpretations of the generalities within the Internal Revenue Code and in subsequent Treasury Department regulations have been exceedingly loose. (Government censorship of foundations does not require additional legislation.) No honestly educational (not to mention charitable) endeavor has been hampered. The Fund for the Republic, the only major foundation created to work exclusively in the sensitive areas of civil liberties and civil rights, weathered successfully more criticisms than most philanthropoids would ever have imagined, and today it supports the highly controversial Center for the Study of Democratic Institutions. The Fund has been investigated and harassed, but it has survived assaults from the most powerful opponents of foundations. IRS guidelines published in 1968 asked foundations merely to present facts on both sides of an issue.

The House tax bill of 1969 called for a ban on attempts by foundations to influence legislation, prohibiting expenditures for political lobbying and electioneering as well as grants to public servants. But it continued to permit support of voter registration drives under certain circumstances, and did not outlaw voter education programs or television shows that were truly educational. During the prolonged debate over tax reform measures no speeches emanated from Congress or the White House calling for the crippling or destruction of foundations. Senator Herman E. Talmadge of Georgia, a member of the Senate Finance Committee, complained that there appeared to have been many abuses of foundation funds: for example, gifts to political officials, including federal judges, and voter registration drives aimed at helping certain candidates. But he made no proposals that would effectively hinder the charitable and legitimately educational activities of foundations.

In short, foundations could surely live and prosper under legislation of this nature; it deprives them of few outlets for their energies or resources. And it does not appear unreasonable, reactionary, or contrary to the public's wishes to keep tax-exempt funds out of the area of clearly partisan politics.

The language of the House bill was flexible enough to preserve the educational and charitable effectiveness of foundations, Treasury Secretary David M. Kennedy argued in September, 1969. "While the line between education and the influencing of legislation may not always be easy to draw, I am confident that the Internal Revenue Service would continue to exercise sound discretion in this respect as it has in the past." [34]

The most thorough and potentially the most significant investigation of foundations has been that started and doggedly pursued for more than eight years by Wright Patman, the septuagenarian Representative from Texarkana, Texas. Patman, a congressman in the Populist tradition, accused foundations of being vast concentrations of wealth controlled largely by easterners, and of being guilty of abusing the sanctuary of tax exemption at the expense of the common man.

[34] G. C. Thelen, Jr., "Nixon Team Split on Foundation Tax," Denver *Post*, September 28, 1969.

24

I do not single out the foundations for harsh regulation—I simply propose that they be subject to the same economic rules as the rest of America. Equal treatment under the law is perhaps a painful contemplation for some of them, but equal treatment under the law is really what America is all about.[35]

While Patman's reports, speeches, and articles are sometimes criticized for their invective and emotionalism, his research has carefully documented numerous examples of the increasingly complex schemes for manipulating foundations for private purposes. Though he may have discovered tactics employed by only a small fraction of foundations, it is just as likely that he has merely scratched the surface of the corruption. The aura of uneasiness and uncertainty in foundation literature since the early 1960's has been due almost entirely to Patman's investigations.

The financial dealings of foundations had drawn attention before Patman's findings. (Business profits have long been the principal source of foundation income. Almost without exception, foundations spend only from their investment income, thus ensuring their own perpetuity and continued financial growth.) In 1944, Congress first required foundations to file information returns so that studies could be made. Six years later, following an investigation of the activities of a business corporation charged with taking financial advantage of a foundation's tax-exempt status, Congress passed the Revenue Act of 1950. This complicated new law added restrictions on foundations and other tax-exempt bodies, such as the prohibition of certain transactions which diverted funds to the donor or his associates. But the key words of the act were imprecise,

---

[35] U.S., Congress, House, Statement by Representative Wright Patman before the House Committee on Ways and Means, 91st Cong., 1st Sess., February 18, 1969, *Congressional Record*, p. H1014.

owing to disagreement over the measure in Congress. When, for example, a foundation earned income from a business activity "not substantially related" to charity and "regularly" carried on, that income was subject to taxation. Higher postwar taxes were diverting great accumulations of wealth to foundations, and the question arose about the amount of principal or income that should be directed to a social purpose in a given year. The 1950 law denied exemptions to foundations withholding sums that were "unreasonable in amount or duration." As Robert Bremner put it, "The legal or not yet prohibited forms of tax benefit enjoyed by foundations remained sufficiently appealing to encourage further growth." [36]

The Cox Committee, stymied in its efforts to gather information quickly on the financial operations of foundations, recommended an amendment to the Revenue Code requiring foundations to disclose to the government such financial data as administrative expenses and accumulations of resources. It also requested the Ways and Means Committee to "reexamine pertinent tax laws" with a view toward increasing the flow of funds to philanthropy.

The Reece Committee offered several proposals for consideration by the Ways and Means Committee, including a denial of tax exemption to any foundation holding more than 5 or 10 per cent of its capital in the securities of a single enterprise, and the mandatory appointment, to every foundation board, of a trustee selected by a government agency.

But no major amendments to the Internal Revenue Code pertaining to foundations were enacted after the 1950 revisions; the effects of the investigations of the early 1950's were largely rhetorical. And then Wright Patman picked up the cudgels.

[36] *American Philanthropy*, p. 175.

Congressman Patman first publicly expressed his dissatisfaction with foundations in a series of speeches before the House in May, 1961. In August he reported that "the mail I have received from all parts of the country, as well as press stories . . . indicate a growing public concern over the lack of adequate regulation of privately controlled, tax-exempt foundations." Later that month he began sending lengthy questionnaires to the larger foundations, announcing: "I am making a study of the impact of foundations on our economy." Following suggestions that a committee of the House ought to be involved in the investigation, Patman declared in early October that the Select Committee on Small Business, of which he was Chairman, had assumed the study. But the probe was, in fact, almost entirely an individual effort.[37]

Patman gathered more facts about foundations than any other congressman had yet been able to. "Never before have the economic factors of the complex and rapidly expanding foundation business been put under the microscope of public scrutiny." [38] In late 1962 he published a report to his committee, containing most of the charges he would level against foundations in six subsequent reports and in two public hearings. Using information received from over 500 foundations, representing approximately 90 per cent of all foundation assets, Patman revealed the numerous and often sophisticated methods by which the prohibitions of the Revenue Act of 1950 were evaded. Foundations had been used to control and

[37] See "Representative Patman Queries Foundations," *Foundation News*, 2 (November, 1961), 3. For an early elaboration by Patman of his view that "foundations have become a force in our society second only to that of Government itself," see "Congressman Discusses Foundations," *ibid.*, 2 (July), 3.

[38] *Tax-Exempt Foundations and Charitable Trusts: Chairman's Report*, p. vi.

enrich businesses, to stifle business competition, to pay large salaries to members of donors' families, to act as loan companies, and to play the stock market. Treasury Department supervision of foundations was described, correctly, as cursory and sporadic.

Among the report's sixteen specific recommendations was a regulatory agency for the supervision of foundations; a national registry of all foundations, to be published annually; a prohibition on all moneylending, borrowing, and business operations by foundations; a twenty-five-year limitation on a foundation's life; a requirement that no income tax deductions be allowed to a foundation until the sum donated was actually contributed to charity; fuller foundation tax returns; and stiff penalties and revocation of tax exemption for improper or insufficient reporting to the federal government.

Patman's report received much publicity and was widely recognized as a generally responsible and long-overdue critique of the financial operations of what was hopefully a small minority of foundations.

Action was not long in coming. In 1962 and 1963 foundation tax forms were revised to include more information. Scheduled audits by the Internal Revenue Service were greatly increased in frequency. Plans were laid for the first published list of all foundations registered with the IRS. In the spring of 1963 the IRS created an Exempt Organization Council, directed to produce policy recommendations. In the same year the Treasury Department named a fourteen-man special Advisory Committee on Foundations to provide the government with information it presumably did not have. (Patman decried the secrecy with which the Committee was appointed, and correctly pointed out that "ten of the fourteen members . . . are tied in with foundations.") [39] The Revenue Act of 1964 imposed higher standards upon foundations seeking to be recipients of unlimited charitable contributions, including a denial of this privilege to foundations which engage in financial transactions with their donors or related parties.

At the request of two congressional committees, the Treasury Department conducted an intensive survey of approximatly 1,300 foundations to gauge the adequacy of the 1950 amendments to the Internal Revenue Code. The Department's 110-page report was published in February, 1965, and contained six proposals—far less radical than Patman's—designed to eliminate certain financial benefits enjoyed by donors who controlled foundations and certain tactics, used with the assistance of foundations, against business competition. In appraising three general criticisms made by Patman, the Treasury study concluded that foundations had been guilty of unnecessarily delaying the use of funds donated for charitable purposes, that they had not become a disproportionately large segment of the national economy, and that no substantial data were discovered to confirm the contention that "foundations represent dangerous concentrations of economic and social power."

The spirit of the report was friendly, far different in tone from Patman's belligerent and sometimes abusive language. The Treasury Department appraisal found indications that "most private foundations act responsibly and contribute sig-

---

[39] *Tax-Exempt Foundations and Charitable Trusts: Their Impact on Our Economy*, (Third Installment), U.S. House of Representatives, 88th Cong., (Washington, D.C.: U.S. Government Printing Office, 1964), p. v.

nificantly to the improvement of our society." It did not recommend a separate federal regulatory agency, nor did it support Patman's recommendation for a time limit on the life of foundations. Changes in the tax laws or Treasury regulations (the report failed to specify which) could be created, it concluded, to curb abuses practiced by a minority of foundations.

Still, there were many factual matters beyond the scope of the study—for example, "the growth of the total wealth of charitable organizations including foundations." The sample used for the survey was small. Statistics came from a single year's operations, and this may have distorted conclusions. Moreover, although the report strongly stressed the value of venture capital, it failed to deal with the issues of the internal, public, and political factors inhibiting meaningful innovation by foundations. It was apparent from this carefully prepared study that there was a need for further research and for more thought about the role and operations of foundations in modern America.[40]

Partially as a result of additional reports compiled under the direction of Representative Patman, and the political groundswell against "tax loopholes," the Treasury Department released in early 1969 a set of proposed reforms for the nation's tax system. Included was a further endorsement to require tax-free groups to be operated separately from businesses and to prevent the creator of a foundation from using it as a resource for his own gains. The Nixon administration gave only halfhearted support to the recommendations (written under the Johnson administration) but pledged to undertake a long-range examination of the entire tax structure.

In April, the administration made public its interim tax re-

[40] See *Treasury Department Report on Private Foundations*, pp. 5–82.

form plan. The proposal called for the creation of specific civil penalties, enforceable in the federal courts, to prevent improper financial dealings by foundations, and the establishment of jurisdiction in the federal courts "to enforce the obligation of a Federally tax-exempt organization—not just foundations—to devote funds properly to charitable purposes." The public demand for a measure of tax equality had not been ignored. "The prospect of a Republican tax reform," Joseph Kraft commented, "is more than just a piece of legislative news. It marks a turning point of historic proportions." [41]

Congressman Wilbur D. Mills, Chairman of the House Ways and Means Committee, announced hearings on comprehensive tax reform proposals, presenting a list of subjects very similar to the topics considered by the Treasury Department. On the first day of the public review Representative Patman was called upon to testify.

The Congressman stated that the value of assets held by the 596 foundations his subcommittee had studied had increased 50 per cent from late 1960 through 1966—from 10.2 billion to 15.1 billion dollars. These same foundations, by the end of 1966, had accumulated 1.9 billion dollars in unspent income. Patman called for a 20 per cent tax on the gross income of foundations (excluding contributions, gifts, and grants received) and declared that he favored requiring foundations to annually distribute their entire net income for philanthropic purposes. "The foundations were created to spend, not to hoard and grow—thus Congress should require them to spend, annually, their net income, and for the purposes for which they were organized." He also revealed that of the 596 foundations, 136 held stock in 288 corporations at the close of

[41] "Nixon Has Opportunity for Real Tax Reform," Denver *Post*, February 10, 1969.

1966, in amounts ranging from 5 to 100 per cent of the outstanding shares of at least one class of stock. The estimated market value of those shares, he said, was 4.9 billion dollars. Not surprisingly, Patman declared his intention to offer legislation limiting any privately controlled foundation from owning more than 3 per cent of the stock of a business. "I do not seek to destroy the foundations, but to reform them." [42]

The bill that passed overwhelmingly in the House in August contained far milder restrictions on foundations than Patman sought, but nevertheless called for several important reforms. A 7.5 per cent levy would be placed on the investment income of foundations—a measure intended to replenish the federal treasury with between 65 and 100 million dollars annually. Foundations were to be required to give away each year a sum equal to their investment income or equal to 5 per cent of their assets, whichever was larger. Stricter prohibitions against "self-dealing" were created, to prevent shady financial operations between foundations and their founders, directors, or major contributors. And the bill would limit to 20 per cent the amount of a corporation's stock that could be held by a foundation and related family members.

In October the Senate Finance Committee made slight changes in several of the House proposals, reduced the tax on investment income by about half, and added a forty-year time limit to the life of foundations (the period would start from the passage of the bill for existing foundations). There were predictions that the Senate would strengthen the Committee's recommendations, and it seemed certain that a fairly

[42] See U.S., Congress, House, Statement by Representative Wright Patman before the House Committee on Ways and Means, 91st Cong., 1st Sess., February 18, 1969, *Congressional Record*, pp. H1014–1017.

strong bill would come out of the conference committee chaired by Congressman Wilbur Mills.

To resist such reforms, foundations waged the most intensive publicity campaign in their history. A parade of spokesmen and partisans appeared before the congressional committees, predicting doom and bankruptcy for foundations. (The President of Notre Dame—a trustee of the Rockefeller Foundation—told the Senate Finance Committee that the 7.5 per cent tax would cut support for education and scientific research by sixty-five million dollars a year immediately and by one hundred million dollars in a few years.) Scores of editorials in major newspapers and magazines charged Congress with endangering the freedom and prosperity of American philanthropy. (One writer in the *Saturday Review* said, "If the tax reform bill . . . now before the Senate Finance Committee should become law in its present form, the golden age of the private philanthropic foundation will come to an end.") [43] In September, several major foundations announced plans for a private agency to set and maintain standards of operation for foundations. The privately supported Commission on Foundations and Private Philanthropy (an idea of John D. Rockefeller III) assured the Senate Finance Committee in late October that there were less extreme alternatives to the proposals passed by the House.

The bill that was signed by the President in December, 1969, included a levy of 4 per cent on annual investment income, strict prohibitions against self-dealing, and a requirement that foundations distribute all of their investment income in the year after it is earned or an amount equal to 6 per

[43] Frank G. Jennings, "Tax Reform and the Foundations," *Saturday Review*, 52 (October 18, 1969), 32. The magazine failed to tell its readers that the author of the article was a foundation consultant.

cent of assets, whichever is larger. Complex restrictions against foundation ownership of businesses were also part of the 1969 Tax Reform Act. In addition, foundations were prohibited from expending funds to "attempt to influence any legislation through an attempt to affect the opinion of the general public or any segment thereof," except when examining "broad, social, economic and similar problems of the type the government could be expected to deal with ultimately, even though this would not permit lobbying on matters which have been proposed for legislative action." Mild restrictions were placed on voter registration drives, and most foundations were required to make full annual reports, which could be made public. A complex formula of taxes for violation of the regulations was made available to the federal government, in addition to the penalty of revocation of tax-exempt status.

To many observers the new act—while clumsy and vague in places—seemed responsible and progressive. Whatever the *potential* dangers of a tax on foundation income (the selection by John W. Gardner speaks particularly to this question), it seems certain that in light of the growing number and growing financial strength of foundations, such a tax—especially of the size determined by Congress in 1969—will in no way imperil the strength of foundations or in itself cause a marked reduction in foundation giving. Nor is there much to condemn in the desire of Congress to increase the amount of money spent by foundations for charitable and educational purposes each year. Foundations have tax-exempt status presumably to encourage giving.

Moreover, a reasonable limit on the life of a foundation does not appear to be likely to endanger charitable endeavors. This regulatory proposal was not included in the 1969 law, but may be raised again. Few programs require more than forty years to reach fruition, long-range projects might secure funds from newer foundations as the years pass, and all assets of a dissolved foundation would revert to charity in any case. The desire of donors and philanthropoids to increase a foundation's wealth indefinitely might well fall short of being an absolute right.

Early in 1970, foundations, notably the larger ones, appeared to be more influential than ever before, an impression strengthened by the movement between government and private philanthropy of such dignitaries as McGeorge Bundy, Dean Rusk, John W. Gardner, David E. Bell, Harold Howe II, and Roger W. Wilkins. Yet there were also strong currents of dissent running against these great corporations and trusts, serious questions raised about their uses and their ultimate usefulness.

In recent years Congress has taken several steps toward cracking down on many of the profit-making devices employed by foundations as well as toward restoring their political neutrality. But these matters, along with the deeper issues of public responsibility and venture capital, may well have to be debated further in Congress, and outside as well. The alarming acceleration of foundation assets will probably induce such confrontations. (Patman's Subcommittee on Foundations intensified its study of foundations following passage of the 1969 tax reform law.) It is hoped that the following selections will both enlighten and inform, and will prompt meaningful and productive discussion.

Part One
Public Responsibility

REECE REPORT ON
TAX-EXEMPT FOUNDATIONS *

THE POWER to allot or distribute substantial funds carries with it the opportunity to exercise a substantial degree of control over the recipients. We tolerate such risks to society in the free and uncontrolled use of private funds. An individual of wealth has wide freedom to expend his money for power or propaganda purposes; in the process, he may obtain control of educational institutions, media of communication and other agencies which have an important impact on society. Distasteful though this may sometimes be, broad freedom to do it is consonant with our general ideas of freedom and liberty for the individual.

When we are dealing with foundations, the situation is quite different. Problems arise in connection with granting full liberty to foundations which increase geometrically with their size. The power of the purse becomes something with which the public must reckon. *For these great foundations are public trusts, employing the public's money—become so*

---

* *Tax-Exempt Foundations: Report of the Special Committee to Investigate Tax-Exempt Foundations and Comparable Organizations*, U.S. House of Representatives, 83d Cong., 2d Sess., House Report No. 2681 (Washington, D.C.: United States Government Printing Office, 1954), pp. 20–22. The Reece Committee's final report, signed by three of the five Committee members, was published December 20, 1954. The late Congressman Reece, from Tennessee, served in the House from 1921–1931, 1935–1947, and 1951–1961. He was Chairman of the Republican National Committee from 1946 to 1948.

through tax exemption and dedication to public purposes. Foundations are permitted to exist by the grace of the public, exempted from the taxation to which private funds are subjected, and are entitled to their privileges only because they are, and must be, dedicated to the public welfare. The public has the right to expect of those who operate the foundations the highest degree of fiduciary responsibility. The fiduciary duty is not merely to administer the funds carefully from a financial standpoint. It includes the obligation to see that the public dedication is properly applied. . . .

Public Accountability

Annual returns are required of the foundations which give certain information to the Federal government. Parts of these reports are open to the public. Others are not: they may be examined only by Executive Order of the President of the United States. Even this Committee . . . has had difficulty in securing such an order; the public in general has no chance of securing one. Thus even the material which by law must now be recorded is not fully open to the public. This Committee fails to understand why any part of any report by a foundation should not be open to the public. Its funds are public and its benefactions, its activities, should be public also. In any event, the report which must be filed is wholly inadequate to enable either government or the public to determine whether a foundation has fulfilled its duty to the public.

Some of the major foundations prepare and issue public reports which are admirable as far as they go, disclosing full financial statements and descriptions of their work during the period covered by the report. But even these are inadequate fully to inform the public of the backgrounds, the motivations, the detail of operation and the results of the activities of the foundations.

While truly full reports would give to those interested an opportunity to be critical, such criticism would be ineffective in most instances. The foundations are free to do as they please with the public funds at their command, so long as they do not transgress certain rules of law which are so general in their terms, and so difficult to interpret except in a few instances, that they are virtually useless as deterrents. Political propaganda, for example, is proscribed. But many foundations *do* engage in active political propaganda, and the present laws cannot stop them.

The testimony of Internal Revenue Commissioner Andrews and Assistant Commissioner Sugarman brought out clearly (1) that the courts have construed the restrictions in the tax law very liberally, perhaps far too liberally; (2) that the Internal Revenue Service has great difficulty in drawing lines; and (3) that it does not have the manpower or the machinery to act as a watchdog to make sure that the law is not violated.

Where the organization claims exemption on the ground that it is "educational" the law requires that it have been organized exclusively for that purpose, yet the word "exclusively" has been weakened by judicial interpretation. Again, the words proscribing political activity provide that it may not use a "substantial" part of its funds in that area. The test is thus quantitative as well as qualitative, and the difficulty in determining the borderlines can well be imagined. The fact is, and this seems to us of enormous importance, that the Internal Revenue Service cannot possibly read all the literature produced or financed by foundations, or follow and check the application of their expenditures. The Commissioner must rely chiefly on complaints by indignant citizens to raise a question in his own mind. Even then, it is difficult for the Service to carry this burden, both from limitations of personnel and budget, and because it is here concerned with an area which requires technical skill not normally to be found in a tax bureau.

Our conclusion is that there is no true public accountability under the present laws.

What is the penalty if, by chance, serious malfeasance is proved—perhaps by substantial grants, for subversive purposes or for active political propaganda? The mere loss of the income tax exemption. That is the sole penalty, other than the loss of the right of future donors to take gift or estate tax exemption on their donations. The capital of the foundation may still be used for a malevolent purpose. The trustees are not subjected to any personal penalty. The fund merely suffers by, thereafter, having to pay income tax on its earnings.

CORPORATION GIVING
IN A FREE SOCIETY *

by Richard Eells

IN VIEW of the public exchanges between the Reece Committee and the foundations, the question arises: how far does the investigative power of legislative bodies reach in the process

* *Corporation Giving in a Free Society* (New York: Harper, 1956; copyright © 1956 by Harper & Row Publishers, Inc.), pp. 63–71. The footnotes for this excerpt have been omitted. In 1956 Richard Eells was manager of Public Relations Research at General Electric. He is currently Adjunct Professor in Business at the Graduate School of Business, Columbia University.

of extracting a public accounting from private foundations? Is the purpose to insure a reasonable disclosure to the public of foundations' finances and their philanthropic endeavors? Or does it really go much farther in the direction of outright public control? What must corporation philanthropy be prepared for in the way of meeting its responsibilities under the head of "public accountability"?

The Reece committee hearings, though conducted under what many regard as conservative auspices, introduced a startling case for a radical departure from free enterprise principles. The view was expressed in these hearings that a philanthropic contribution somehow enters the public domain and thus loses its character as private property. . . .

This observation is of more than passing interest to corporation donors. Corporations may ask where the "donated dollars employed by the Fund [for the Advancement of Education] for its teacher-training project came from: the earnings of the Ford Motor Company, or the public treasury? More generally, the issue is this: when corporations make charitable contributions from net earnings, are they spending public money, or their own? Can we assume, without argument, that a certain percentage of undistributed earnings of business corporations—the specific percentage depending upon the federal corporate income-tax rate of the moment—are already in the public domain, and that since a certain part of these earnings is releasable by the corporation under the tax-exemption clauses only under such terms and conditions as Congress may specify, Congress therefore has the power to supervise and control these charitable expenditures? In other words, is corporation philanthropy to be regarded as a kind of delegation of public power over "public funds" to the private management of corporations and corporate foundations, with a reservation of public authority to step in at any time to control that private management of so-called "public funds"?

And if critics dislike the subject matter of a particular foundation project, will this also provide an argument for government control? Turn, for example, to Chairman Reece's adverse comments on such a foundation-sponsored project as the Kinsey study. ". . . It is certainly a project that I . . . that the Government itself would not undertake to make the funds available to sponsor. . . . Then why should some agency whose funds are made available by the Government foregoing the taxes in turn to sponsor a project that has at least such a great question and aura of mystery surrounding it?" Although one committee member seemed to find the very discussion of the Kinsey report a repugnant subject, the logical conclusion of Mr. Reece's uncompleted syllogism would seem to require a thorough airing of this and countless other foundation projects, to make sure that Congress would have supported them directly, rather than indirectly by "public funds privately managed."

Is it true that a corporation has no business granting any of its tax-exempt contributions for purposes which Congress would not approve funds for? Does a corporation have to establish that any scientific, educational, or charitable activities it desires to sponsor would get Congressional appropriations if they came up in an appropriation bill? Is a corporation really handling "public funds" when it takes a deduction for tax-exemption purposes? If so, may Congress set up procedures for pre-audit of the expenditure of such funds?

The committee did not draw the ultimate conclusion to this line of reasoning. Nowhere, apparently, did it really come to grips with the basic issue. No proposal for regulatory legislation over foundations has been forthcoming from either the Reece or Cox committees, though the tightening up of tax-exemption clauses has been recommended to avoid tax avoidance in cases of pseudo-philanthropic gifts. . . .

How, for example, can one measure the "promise" of a project? Can there be no risks, no scientific ventures, no long-range experimental programs with foundation funds derived from tax-exempt contributions? By what standards does one compare the ordinary business return with the immeasurable benefits of a corporate contribution to a community fund, a liberal arts college, or a research institution? Why limit a corporate donor to "nation-as-a-whole" benefits, when the immediate requirements of the local plant communities may reasonably be put first on the list? How, indeed, can corporation philanthropy live in a legal atmosphere that poses two contradictory requirements: that the contribution bear some reasonable relation to the corporation's own interests and the interests of its stockholders; and that, on the other hand, it show irrefutably in advance a benefit to the nation as a whole rather than to any part of it?

Public Accountability: Some Prospects

The shortcomings of the Reece investigation results are clear. What is not so clear is the future of corporate accountability for corporation philanthropy. It is possible that the public will demand more rigorous control of foundations and charitable trusts through extensive federal and state legislation. More probable, if foundations and trusts are wisely managed and their philanthropic programs are creatively developed, is the emergence of *a voluntary system of public accountability*.

Corporate donors have an important stake in the develop-

45

ment of such a voluntary system, not only for corporation philanthropy but for foundations generally. The importance of this may not be widely recognized. The need for moving ahead on a broad front is inescapable. The recent investigations concentrated upon the older foundations; they devoted little attention to the new growth of corporation foundations. In time, these too will be brought under the legislators' microscope. They will, that is to say, unless the corporate donors themselves undertake the task of ensuring that their programs meet the standards of adequate public accountability.

But it is not merely the negative avoidance of legislative controls that should motivate the creation of such a voluntary system. On the positive side, corporate donors have much to gain through the initiation of procedures for squaring their philanthropic designs with generally acceptable community values. . . . It does not have to be assumed that the objectives of corporation philanthropy must swing with every breeze. There is "a *deliberate* sense of the community," as Senator J. William Fulbright remarked recently, which expects something more of its leaders. They are expected rather to guide, teach, and counsel "the community at large as it seeks on its own to know, and then to do the good." The venture capital of corporate philanthropy can best be used by those leaders who are willing to accept such responsibilities for frontier work, much of which may not be immediately understood.

Public accountability for corporation philanthropy can be looked upon as an onerous task; or it can be regarded more affirmatively as an opportunity for opening new avenues of rapport between the corporation and its public environment. The positive approach to public accountability for corporation giving will commend itself to business leaders. If and when they do determine to take this position in working out a voluntary system, there are at least four means they will find worthy of exploration.

First, corporate donors will seek the common ground for all philanthropy, whether through the older foundations and trusts or through the newer corporation foundations. Tendencies toward isolation and separatism can defeat cooperative efforts to build up sound bases for a voluntary system of public accountability. So long as the corporation foundation is regarded as *sui generis,* a separate breed, having little in common with others who work in the field, it will be dfficult to establish communication among responsible leaders in philanthropic work. The need is for organized collaboration in developing effective ways of sensing the public interest, designing philanthropic programs that will promote the general welfare, and reporting continuously to the community what is being done.

Second, private philanthropic foundations can set up their own investigating committees to discover trends, problems, points of friction, areas of unsatisfactory performance, and unfulfilled responsibility among the foundations. This may seem to be a counsel of perfection. The foundations, it may be objected, will be the last to point a finger of criticism at their own shortcomings; they will never be persuaded to police themselves as a group. Possibly this is true; but one wonders how many more Reece investigations will be needed to bring home the point. Critics of the Reece proceedings may still entertain doubts that foundations as a whole are doing the kind of job they can do and ought to do—as private, autonomous organs. Certainly corporation philanthropy has everything to gain and little to lose by opening its doors to public inspection carried on under the frendly auspices of its fellow-toilers in the field. Self-investigation on a quadrennial or decennial basis should not be an impossible pattern.

Third, the designs of methods of *continuous* public accountability requires cooperative effort among the foundations. There is need for a "clearing house" type of operation, supported by modest contributions from all the foundations and charitable trusts. Here there could be a pooling of experience with various ways of setting standards for philanthropic work, measuring foundation performance, and conducting post-audits of programs actually carried out. In addition, there could be an interchange of knowledge concerning prevailing standards of public policy as to foundation practice. Trends of public opinion—the inchoate stage of public policy formation—could likewise be assessed. The recent hearings contain some evidence that foundations have a special public relations problem, or perhaps more accurately a problem of establishing satisfactory and continuing relationships with certain special publics.

Fourth, the form of reporting to the public by individual corporate donors can be improved. It is inconceivable, for example, that public accountability for corporation philanthropy can properly be confined to a few sentences in a corporation's annual report to its stockholders. Corporate donors do have a responsibility to the stockholders to make a full accounting of the objectives, the programs, and the achievements of their corporate giving. But beyond this, media must be used for reaching other and broader publics. This task will demand the best efforts of an able public relations staff.

FOUNDATION FUNDS—
WHOSE MONEY? *

by F. Emerson Andrews

IN THE press, and occasionally in the halls of Congress, one hears the statement that the funds of foundations are "public money," with the implication that they are built up largely from tax savings which otherwise would have flowed into the public coffers, and therefore "the public"—presumably through its elected representatives—should have the right to dictate how these funds are spent. . . .

What are the facts? The question needs to be examined on two bases: first, exemption of foundations themselves, with respect to their own income; secondly, deductibility to donors, individual or corporate, with respect to their contributions to foundations. . . .

As the corporation income tax is presently at the rate of 52 per cent, and the combined income of all the foundations is in the neighborhood of $700 million annually, it is commonly assumed that foundation exemption from corporate income tax results in a loss of hundreds of millions of dollars in federal revenue. This is not true. Since the 1950 revision of the Code, taxing the unrelated business operations of foundations, the remaining exemption is fiscally negligible.

* "Foundation Funds—Whose Money?" *Foundation News*, 4 (January, 1963), 5–7. F. Emerson Andrews is the foremost authority on private tax-exempt foundations. He was the first Director of the Foundation Library Center and remains on the Center's board of trustees. He is the author of several books and numerous articles on tax-exempt corporations and trusts.

If tomorrow every philanthropic foundation were ruled subject to full taxation, the increase in federal revenue would be slight. Foundations are organized as corporations or as trusts. With respect to the former, the 52 per cent corporate tax is levied, not on gross income, but on net profit. The operating foundation that spends all its income on projects and administrative costs has obviously no profit on which to be taxed. There is at least a legal case that the grant-making foundation is pursuing its "business" in making grants, and if it disburses its total income, as most of them do, it also has no profits on which to be taxed. An adverse decision by the courts would bring pressure upon foundations to become operating organizations.

But even an adverse decision would not result in any substantial tax upon incorporated foundations. . . . In the first place, they would be exempt, as are all business corporations, on 85 per cent of income from dividends of other corporations. Capital gains tax, to which some would be subject, is at a maximum of 25 per cent. Administrative costs would be deductible, and range generally from 4 to about 14 per cent of total income. Additionally, they could deduct, as can all business corporations, a maximum of 5 per cent of net income given to charitable causes. For many foundations the taxable balance would approach or reach zero. Moreover, the rate for corporations is 30 per cent, not 52 per cent, on the first $25,-000 of taxable income.

With respect to foundations organized as trusts, a comparable result obtains. Under IRC Sec. 642 (c) an estate or trust (exemption is not pertinent) may deduct without limitation amounts "paid or permanently set aside" for charitable purposes. The removal of exemption, therefore, would under present law bring into the federal treasury negligible income from either incorporated or trust-type foundations. . . .

Tax "exemption" is in some respects a misnomer. Government at its various levels has the right to impose taxes. In the light of varying and usually increasing needs for revenue, government from time to time levies taxes upon selected segments of the economy. Examples are profit-making corporations, individuals, estates, donors of large gifts, travelers, theater-goers, purchasers of alcohol, tobacco, gasoline, and in some states consumers generally.

The absence of a tax which legally could be levied does not make those untaxed funds "public money." Mr. John D. Rockefeller, Jr., is reported to have been angered by this suggestion. He pointed out that the government had the legal power to tax 100 per cent of his income. But since it did leave a part to him to spend, he regarded this remainder as his money, and in no sense public.

Somewhat similarly, organizations of the foundation type never have been taxed—unless they fell under special provisions of the Code due to prohibited transactions, unreasonable accumulation, or similar activities. When the Revenue Act of 1894 sought to impose the first tax on corporate profits, the levy was upon "all corporations organized for profit." The omission of charitable organizations was obvious in that language, but was also made explicit in this proviso:

That nothing herein contained shall apply to . . . corporations, companies, or associations organized and conducted solely for charitable, religious, or educational purposes.

This tax measure was declared unconstitutional, but the same provisions appeared in the 1909 legislation, which be-

51

came the first general tax measure affecting corporations. They have been carried, in gradually expanding form, in all subsequent federal tax codes; foundations were first specifically mentioned in 1921. . . . With minor exceptions, charitable, educational, and religious organizations never have been taxed on their general income in the United States.

Why have the taxing authorities not levied taxes directly on these types of organizations? Even more significantly, why have they encouraged gifts to them from individuals, corporations, and estates, by making such gifts deductible from taxed income?

The first and most frequent argument is that educational and charitable agencies perform functions that would otherwise have to be performed by government, so that there is an effective *quid pro quo*. As a corollary, it is sometimes asserted that these organizations perform such functions more efficiently and at less cost than they could have been performed by government.

The motivation must be broader than this, however. Some agencies serve the public welfare in areas beyond any present government activity, or even in areas forbidden to government—e.g., support of religion. These tax inducements encourage support for a wide variety of voluntary agencies that fill gaps in, or perform functions inappropriate for, government services.

Freedom to experiment and wide dispersion of decision-making are also results of general tax encouragement, as opposed to specific governmental grants or direct operation. . . .

With respect to religious and certain other types of organizations, a further motive in tax exemption has been advanced. The power to tax is the power to destroy. Since religious freedom is a Constitutional guarantee, that freedom should not be endangered by granting taxing powers to government in sensitive areas.

Throughout American history philanthropic organizations have in general gone untaxed, both at the federal and the state and local levels. For most of these organizations, even if they were to be treated as business corporations or nonexempt trusts, the federal taxes on income would under present laws be fiscally unimportant.

Vastly more important to these organizations is the privilege of deductibility on contributions made to them. In this case the actual savings in tax payments flow to the contributors, but the result is undoubtedly substantially to increase the flow of funds to the "exempt" organizations. The public policy involved appears to include the recognition that some of the funds so gathered will reduce expenditures by government for the same purposes; a desire to encourage a wider range of welfare activities than would be possible or appropriate for government; a wish to decentralize power and to distribute decision-making; a hope that experimentation may be stimulated; and a desire to protect sensitive areas against possible punitive taxation.

The moneys not taxed away, and the more substantial sums drawn into these welfare organizations by the inducements of deductibility, are indeed moneys affected with the public interest; they must be spent for welfare purposes and not for private advantage, and their use should be open to full public scrutiny. But they are not "public funds" subject to public controls any more than similar sums given to a church, school, or hospital. One does not hear loud argument that the tax-deductible funds given to churches lay upon them a responsibility to teach only doctrines that "the public currently wishes, approves and likes." Religious freedom has been won, though at times it may need to be defended; it is less certain that the battle for intellectual freedom has been won along the broad fronts over which foundations operate.

REPORT OF THE PRESIDENT OF THE CARNEGIE CORPORATION, 1968 *

by Alan Pifer

THE FOUNDATION is, paradoxically, both private and public in its nature. It is private because it is incorporated as a private, nongovernmental institution, derives its assets from private donors, and is privately controlled by a donor-appointed or self-perpetuating board of trustees.

There is a common misunderstanding that the public character of the foundation, and hence the public stake in it, derives from its tax-exempt status. How frequently has one heard it said that foundations are really spending public money, and therefore should be subject to greater governmental control. Such a view, however, is based on fallacious reasoning and reveals either surprising ignorance or a dangerous disavowal of one of the basic tenets of the American system.

Throughout our history we have believed in pluralism and have practiced it. We have recognized that the nation's public purposes are considerably more extensive in scope than its governmental purposes, and, through the aegis of the state, we

---

* "The Report of the President," *Annual Report for the Fiscal Year Ended September 30, 1968* (New York: Carnegie Corporation, 1968), pp. 5-6, 10-13. Alan Pifer was appointed President of the Carnegie Corporation in May, 1967.

have enabled a wide variety of private institutions, including foundations, to be chartered to accomplish certain *public,* though *nongovernmental,* purposes. We have also, through the aegis of the state, given tax exemption to these institutions to facilitate their work and have regarded this as being eminently in the public interest. Therefore, to attribute the public stake in the foundation to its tax-exempt status or to regard this status as a "privilege" is wholly erroneous. It is, in Professor Milton Katz's pithy phrase, "to mistake an effect for a cause."

The true origin of the public aspect of the foundation lies in the nature of its activity. It is public because it devotes its funds to purposes in which the total society has a vital interest, such as education, health, and welfare. Grants in these fields do without question affect the public, and hence the public has a legitimate stake in the foundations which make them.

But there is an even more important sense in which the foundation is public in character. It is public because the public cannot afford to regard with indifference how foundation funds are spent, so precious are they, as we have seen, in the vital process of social change, and so limited are they in amount. The $1.3 billion spent by foundations in 1967 was, for example, less than 0.2 per cent of the Gross National Product, less than 9 per cent of total voluntary giving, and only 3 per cent of the federal government's expenditure for health, education, and welfare.

Foundation funds, in short, offer a case where a technically private asset is of such potential value to the nation that it must, perforce, be regarded as a public asset. The implications of this proposition are far reaching. . . .

In the popular mind, the term accountability usually has the restricted meaning of answerability for fiscal regularity in the handling of funds over which one has stewardship. In government it has come to have a wider meaning which includes fiscal regularity but also connotes answerability for adherence to budgetary prescriptions and for efficiency in administration. In the professions, for example medicine or law, accountability implies conformity to certain customary and statutory standards, basically of an ethical nature. Accountability can be of a well-defined, direct, or immediate sort, as to a superior within an administrative hierarchy, or it can be indirect, undefined, or even quite vague—something one simply feels as a consequence of his own professional, moral, or ethical standards. Finally, it can apply either to individuals or collectively to organizations. In all cases it implies the obligation to be prepared to give reasons for and explanations of one's conduct to the public.

There are already in existence several forms of public accountability by foundations, some of which are outside foundation control and some of which are within their control. Among the former the most important is the federal requirement that foundations, in consideration of their tax exemption, file a report annually with the Internal Revenue Service. This report, known as Form 990-A, includes information on income, disbursements, administrative expenses, assets and liabilities, as well as other pertinent matters such as whether any funds have been used to influence legislation or participate in a political campaign. Information in this form, with one exception, is made available to the public. The annual submission of Form 990-A to the federal government is important but is, of course, restricted in the purpose it can serve to the relevant provisions of the Internal Revenue Code. With state regulation . . . it constitutes the only form of governmentally imposed public accountability by foundations and is strictly limited in nature.

A second external form of public accountability by foundations is press comment. Theoretically, this could be a powerful instrument for calling foundations to the bar of an informed public opinion. In fact, the press has generally not shown itself to be well informed or sophisticated in its treatment of foundations. Major exceptions can, of course, be found here and there among writers for certain newspapers, news magazines, and journals of opinion. Blame must also be placed on the foundations themselves. Some have actively, even brusquely, discouraged press interest and others have refrained from trying to interest the press in their activities because of an old-fashioned and virtuous, but perhaps optimistic, belief that good works should be done in secret and will in time provide their own advertisement.

Among internal forms of accountability, there is the type provided by organizations which the foundation field has itself created, chiefly the Foundation Library Center and the Council on Foundations. The former, though having other functions, is essentially what its name implies, a library. The latter is a membership organization open to any grant-making foundation. Both are supported by foundation contributions. Through their meetings, counseling services, research, and publications, these two organizations help to raise standards in the field.

The Council, which has a broad membership of all types of foundations—general purpose, community, family and corporate, both American and Canadian—serves as a general forum for the exchange of views among foundation officers and trustees. The Library Center, by means of the current *Foundation Directory* which it prepares, its collection of annual reports and other reference materials, and its willingness to answer enquiries, provides the public with a readily available source of information about foundations. With headquarters in New York City and a branch in Washington, D.C., it maintains depositories in seven locations in other parts of the country.

But neither of these organizations (valuable as they are, is in a position to criticize foundations directly and specifically by name. Their suggestions and exhortations have to be broad and general in nature, and experience shows that the foundations which could profit most from such criticism are least likely to listen to it.

A second internal form of accountability, tenuous and subtle in nature but nonetheless real, is that imposed on foundations by the concern which their staffs are likely to have for their own professional reputations. These concerns are of two quite different kinds: a desire for distinction as a foundation practitioner, wise, skilled, and fairminded in discerning the public interest, and for professional recognition within a discipline. Of the two the former is probably the more important to the public. The latter, if it assumes too great importance to a foundation officer, can even be antithetical to the public interest because it may diminish the officer's capacity to recognize the general good and to give this precedence over the special, and sometimes selfish, interests of a particular discipline or profession. This form of accountability is, of course, limited by the failure of many foundations to employ any professional staff at all, a shortcoming which many informed people regard as one of the principal liabilities of the foundation field.

A third and extremely important internal medium for public accountability is provided by foundation boards of trustees, whose principal duty as directors of a philanthropic agency is to serve the public interest and have a sense of obligation for accountability to the public. But, paradoxically, the trustees are also there to carry on the donor's interests, and, as time goes by and conditions change, these may well begin to fall a good deal short of what independent observers would then consider to be of greatest benefit to the public. Nonetheless, the trustees, out of loyalty to the donor, or a sense of obligation to him or his family, may be reluctant to change with the times. . . .

There is also the problem of board composition. If trustees have a responsibility to serve the public interest, should they then be so selected as to be representative of the public? Foundations have been equivocal on this question. Some have denied the need for representatives and have taken the view that trustees can best serve the general interest precisely by not being representative of special interests. Others have taken tentative steps to provide broader representation in their boards but have not admitted the principle in full. It remains an area of confusion and is one that will probably become increasingly troublesome.

Taking the field at large, one would have to question whether there is to be found today in most foundation boards an adequate variety of trustee experience with current problems of the society. A study of board membership would probably reveal that trustees are largely drawn from the same social class, the same age group, the same professions, the same educational background, the same sex, and the same race.

A final internal form of public accountability is provided by the annual reports which some foundations publish voluntarily. These reports usually include a list of trustees and senior staff, a description of the foundation's program interests, a list of its donations for the past year including the purpose, recipient, and amount of each grant, and a complete financial statement including a breakdown of administrative expenses. Unfortunately, although the issuing of such a report is a basic canon of good foundation practice, most foundations still fail to comply with it. Of the 249 foundations with assets of over $10 million, less than a third have ever issued a report and fewer than a quarter do so regularly each year. Various excuses for not publishing reports have been advanced by foundations over the years, none of them convincing. The record has improved slightly with time but is still reprehensible.

Potentially, there is no more important form of accountability than these published reports, especially were they to include some explanation of how the foundation sees its particular program of grants serving the public interest and specifically the public interest as it relates to social change. This, of course, amounts to asking foundations to expose themselves to the full glare of public scrutiny and possibly of public censure or ridicule as well as approbation. But it is not too much for society to expect, and perhaps even require, in return for the unusual freedom which it gives to foundations.

Part Two
Venture Capital

THE ROLE OF PHILANTHROPY:
AN INSTITUTIONAL VIEW *

by Albert M. Sacks

IT IS paradoxical that philanthropy, which traces its lineage through the centuries, should be thought to need a clearer statement of its role. Yet large foundations, whose charters broadly refer them to "charitable" or "educational" purposes, seem intermittently to cast about for some general framework in which to function. Congressional committees have in the past decade embarked upon investigations of whether charitable organizations are abusing their mandates, and have found a definition of those mandates to be an elusive goal, for they are multifarious and changing.

It is dangerous to assume that this has not always been so, but we can identify significant recent departures from the past. The sheer increase in total funds made available by an affluent society brings philanthropy into greater prominence. Far more dramatic has been the emergence of the large foundation, commanding vast resources and testing somewhat uncomfortably under a resultant public attention. These large foundations, with funds that enable them to act upon a scale

* "The Role of Philanthropy: An Institutional View," *Virginia Law Review*, 46 (April, 1960), 516–524, 526–528. The footnotes have been omitted. Albert M. Sacks is a Professor of Law at Harvard University and a member of the District of Columbia and Massachusetts Bars.

not previously possible, have been leaders in the search for new ways in which philanthropy may serve useful purposes. It is this latter development, perhaps more than any other, which has stimulated a fresh look at philanthropy's role.

It is not suggested here that we examine whether philanthropy has affirmative values in our society. At least with respect to those activities which all regard as philanthropic, this would be tantamount to an inquiry into the values of motherhood. Certain tenets have enjoyed such wide and deeply held acceptance over the years that they may safely be taken for granted. And philanthropy is usually defined in precisely those terms which command universal acceptance:

In its simplest definition, philanthropy is the 'love of mankind, especially as manifested in deeds of practical beneficence.' It is that kind of 'good will to men' which induces people to give voluntarily of their money, property, time, and strength to cooperative causes and institutions which serve the welfare, the health, the character, the mind, the soul, and the advancing culture of the human race.

Although the courts have had to decide literally thousands of individual cases by determining whether or not a particular activity or objective is "charitable," they have not developed more precise criteria. The Restatement of Trusts, summarizing the fruits of judicial thought, defines charitable trusts in terms of charitable purposes, and then goes on to say:

A purpose is charitable if its accomplishment is of such social interest to the community as to justify permitting the property to be devoted to the purpose in perpetuity.

This broad definition does not mean, however, that the whole area is shrouded in uncertainty. From the many decisions a number of broad sectors of clearly philanthropic activities have emerged, including "(a) the relief of poverty; (b) the advancement of education; (c) the advancement of religion; (d) the promotion of health; [and] (e) governmental or municipal purposes." But these exemplary areas do not exhaust the concept of philanthropy. Many other activities qualify as "charitable" within the Restatement's definition, and in light of their variety, Professor Scott, the reporter, has concluded that "there is no fixed standard to determine what purposes are of such social interest to the community [as to justify treating them as charitable]: the interests of the community vary with time and place."

Recognition that the concept of philanthropy is relative and dynamic rather than absolute and immutable yields several significant implications. On the one hand, there can be no flat objection to a foundation's new program merely because it represents a departure from established forms and is therefore somewhat unique. On the other hand, we can expect any new program to encounter a suspicious, resistant attitude until it receives community acceptance over a period of time—that is, until it becomes traditional. Even though two activities may both be regarded as charitable, one may be more clearly so than the other. Thus, in the law of charitable trusts, the usual requirements of a "sufficiently large or indefinite class" of beneficiaries is relaxed only in favor of those charities relating to poverty, religion, education, and health. The predilections of the Congress were reflected in its increasing the charitable deduction from twenty to thirty per cent, limited, however, to religious organizations, educational institutions of formal instructions, and hospitals. Here, then, we have one underlying source of the difficulty which a foundation may meet when it strikes out into relatively new fields, such as the financing of social science research.

If identification of "clearly philanthropic" activities is only of limited value with respect to the more marginal areas, our understanding of philanthropy may be aided by an institutional inquiry. What follows is a schematic presentation which is inevitably simplified, but which seems to provide a useful framework for analysis.

Human activities, which are of such communal importance that they should be not only permitted but strongly encouraged, may be carried on by three broad forms of social organization in our society: (1) they may be conducted for private profit through the mechanism of the commercial market; (2) they may be carried on by government; or (3) they may be fostered by a philanthropic organization. This seems obvious enough, but there is a corollary which may not be as clear. Since all three institutional forms conduct activities of great "social interest to the community," philanthropy is not defined distinctively by this or similar phrases. In any event, this trichotomy suggests a variety of fruitful questions.

As an historical matter, what sphere of responsibility has philanthropy evolved in relation to the other two institutions? Has it overlapped them or occupied a distinctive place? Can we identify criteria by reference to which the "appropriateness" of the development has been judged? What is the situation today? Can we, by reference to history or to institutional characteristics, identify the functions that philanthropy is distinctively fitted to perform, as compared with the other two? Full answers to these questions obviously cannot be attempted here, but a provocative beginning is ventured.

A philanthropy is conceived of as a nonbusiness, i.e., nonprofit, and nongovernmental person or group. Of course, it normally invests its funds to secure income in the business market, and it may finance some portion of its activity by a charge for the benefits it confers. It commonly receives financial aid through grants from business and tax advantages from government. Cooperation of philanthropy and government in a single undertaking is becoming more and more common, although we can ordinarily identify the part played by each institution. Classification by form of social organization is not pure, but it is significant.

Why has philanthropic activity been limited to the nonprofit area? To some this question is silly; they note that philanthropy is a working reflection of altruism, of "love of mankind," and therefore intrinsically inconsistent with private profit. Moreover, such special benefits as a tax exemption or permission to devote property in perpetuity should not be granted any activity yielding a profit; otherwise all useful businesses may demand one. Thus it is that the so-called proprietary hospitals operated for profit are not philanthropic, though they may confer the same benefits on the community that other hospitals do. Of course, the distinction cannot arise with respect to such a traditionally philanthropic activity as relief of poverty, wherein talk of private profit is a contradiction in terms.

The basic explanation, however, may go somewhat deeper than altruistic motive. If we imagine a donation for the purpose of supplying free clothing to all young people in the community without regard to wealth, we have a different situation from those described. This is a function which has traditionally been carried on through the commercial market, and gifts of property to conduct such activities on a nonprofit basis have been rare. Such few as have been made have been thought invalid. Yet it is indeed difficult to say that such a gift would not substantially benefit the community. I would suggest as an explanation that when activities have been adjudged

67

adequately performed through the market mechanism, they have not been regarded as philanthropic, even though organized on a nonprofit basis.

If this explanation is sound, it suggests that philanthropy has evolved as an adjunct of, as a supplement to, our economic system of private enterprise, and that it has been thought more naturally suited to those areas where the commercial market does not operate satisfactorily to supply social needs. It should be added that, whether the theory is right or wrong in explaining the limits of power of charitable institutions, donors have not generally made bequests to foster traditionally "business" activities on a nonprofit basis. This general conception of the appropriate roles of business and philanthropy seems to have prevailed for at least the past two or three centuries.

Our present day attitude appears to mark no sharp break with past tradition, but one may discern a quickening tempo in the role of philanthropy, a greater willingness to assume new tasks accompanied by less reluctance on the part of official organs to conclude that commercial enterprise cannot discharge the entire burden. The allocation of television stations for educational purposes during the infancy of the industry is one indicator; philanthropic activities in housing and urban renewal may be another. The motivation for this changed view is unclear. As living standards rise, community needs become more complex, and more of them must be collectively, rather than individually, satisfied. The market mechanism may be seen as less suitable for these changing purposes than heretofore.

In any event, the result has been an increasing overlap between business and charitable activity. Traditionally, we have had the charitable and proprietary school and hospital functioning in fields in some parts of which profit was possible, but wherein the commercial market had not completely fulfilled felt needs. The currently increasing overlap has brought sharpening conflict. On the one hand, Congress has reflected the fear that nonprofit enterprise may by "unfair" competition displace legitimate commercial activity. Thus, charitable operation of an unrelated business, with all income going to charity, has been declared taxable. On the other hand, as the line between philanthropy and business shifts, an increased degree of competition becomes inevitable. The presence of commercial enterprises in a particular field cannot of itself preclude the intrusion of charitable enterprises. Consider the growth in recent years of research laboratories of both kinds.

If the commerical mechanism proves inadequate, there is ordinarily an alternative to private philanthropy in the form of governmental operation. Religious matters must remain in the private domain except for government fringe benefits, but as to most other activities a choice exists. This choice is made by governmental officials, either legislative or executive. On what basis has an allocation of competencies been made?

One congressional committee, in explaining why the tax deduction was limited to gifts made to domestic organizations, asserted that government saves money when a function is privately performed which the government would otherwise pay for, and that the tax benefit is a *quid pro quo* on which the government has a net gain. This explanation is most unsatisfying. The committee may have been implying that it is a matter of indifference whether the activity is private or governmental; the tax benefit is merely a transfer of funds to the unit which happens to perform the service. It is doubtful that the tax exemption historically developed as an alternative to government expenditure. Charities entered upon activities decades and even centuries before government action was thought of as appropriate.

Alternatively, the congressional committee may have been saying that private action is better because it enables government to achieve a lower budget. For some this reward is sufficient, and they would perhaps support the result by asserting that private action is generally superior to public. During the nineteenth century a fairly strong presumption in favor of private action prevailed, and some states even inaugurated a system of regular payments to private agencies for their work. This attitude is not entirely dissipated today, but government is far readier to examine the question of whether public or private action is superior. The quest—surely a legitimate one—is for particulars concerning the merits.

The British confronted the issue in rather sharply etched form a few years ago when they contemplated the place of philanthropy in the "welfare state." After study, a royal commission issued the so-called Nathan Report which arrived at general conclusions deserving careful attention. Noting that private philanthropy had sought to provide "universal services" for deserving economic and social needs, the report concluded that this had been a "magnificent failure" and that the state gradually had broadened its activities from merely filling gaps left by private charity to taking over primary responsibility. The report then turned to the function which might now be performed by "voluntary organization":

The advantage of voluntary effort over state activity lies in its greater flexibility; its ability to set new standards or to undertake new work on its own volition, and without seeking fresh statutory powers; its ability to pioneer; to make additional or more special provision for people suffering from certain types of disadvantages or disabilities; or for young people of exceptional promise; to work outwards from the individual in need of help to the services he needs rather than by the reverse process of discovering the individual in providing a service (we have in mind particularly the case work agencies); to attract to it men and women with a high sense of dedication ready and willing to give themselves to taxing and specially difficult work. We will not enlarge on these virtues, which few would deny. Some of the most valuable activities of voluntary societies consist, however, in the fact that they are able to stand aside from and criticise state action, or inaction, in the interests of the inarticulate man-in-the-street. This may take the form of helping individuals to know and obtain their rights. It also consists in a more general activity of collecting data about some point where the shoe seems to pinch or a need remains unmet. The general machinery of democratic agitation, deputations, letters to the Press, questions in the House, conferences and the rest of it, may then be put into operation in order to convince a wider public that action is necessary.

The Nathan Report, however, made no effort to demark areas appropriate for state and for private action. The commission conceded that "exactly what functions should be undertaken by the state and what by voluntary agencies is a complicated question. . . ."

The listed values inherent in private action surely extend beyond the social welfare field, and are likely to be even more important elsewhere. It remains an open question whether, in the United States, government will shift from filling gaps to taking principal responsibility in such areas as health and higher education with their heavy research and scholarship demands. Where the required fiscal resources plainly exceed those available to private groups, and where there is need of powers of compulsion to secure total or uniform participation —as with a comprehensive system of minimum old age pensions—government is very likely to displace private action, though leaving it room to deal with remaining fringe problems. Here philanthropy runs its course by calling attention to the problem until it is publicly recognized, by pioneering in efforts to deal with it, and then by giving way to government. The inadequacies of philanthropy overshadow its virtues, and it must in the end rest content with "capillary" action.

In other fields, where its distinctive values are greatly prized and cannot readily be duplicated by government, philanthropy should retain at least a major role, and often the dominant one. Wherever initiative of thought and action is valued, wherever a diversity of views and approaches is thought necessary, wherever experimentation in new untried ventures is sought, the many-centered, disorderly, and even "irresponsible" private groups must be relied upon. Herein lie fundamental values. The compulsions and uniformities of government become a positive drawback. It would be unfortunate, for example, to have government play an exclusive or even dominant operational role in social science research. Where private action has unique advantages but funds available only to government are needed, the no longer novel government grant may be invoked.

The matter, however, ought not to be regarded as a struggle for supremacy between philanthropy and government. Each should be free to try its hand and to make its contribution. It is unlikely, despite the all-or-nothing views of polemic writings, that one will totally displace the other in any field. Through trial and experience a division and accommodation of functions will eventually emerge, albeit subject to further change, which will enable each institution to play the part it does best. Surely, some such process must be taking place in the overwhelmingly important task of aiding underdeveloped areas in which business, philanthropy, and government are all playing a role. A study of this and similar developments should make a significant contribution to our understanding of this process.

The resulting relationships need not be tidy. Symmetrical allocation is not the aim. Rather it is to assure that the welfare state be made compatible with the freedoms of a pluralistic society. . . .

If public regulation were to take the form of detailed and pervasive standards dictating the purposes and methods of operation of each charity, the cure might well be worse than the disease. The basic institutional values of philanthropy—freedom to try new and experimental programs, diversity of approaches, multiple centers of initiative—would probably be seriously diluted, if not destroyed. Apart from minimum standards of bona fide operation, can government officials regulate the efficiency and effectiveness of philanthropic activities without effectively taking them over? It is feasible to impose upon charities the duties of trustees acting for individual beneficiaries to the extent that the two are comparable. This would reach, for example, improper investment of funds and self dealing. But with respect to the vital activity of a charity, the discharge of its purpose, one may doubt that an effective line can be drawn beyond that of good faith. Even a test of reasonable prudence must be qualified by recognition that philanthropic organizations often cannot be judged by the same standards as business firms. Freed from the profit mechanism, they may legitimately view as part of their function the risking of funds on daring experiments, many of which are expected to fail or to succeed only in part.

It is for these reasons that "publicity" is frequently advanced as the most promising mode of regulation. What is meant by "publicity" is often not clear. Presumably, the charity is to be required to disclose facts concerning its operations through registration and periodic reports. There remain, however, two difficult problems: (1) What facts are to be disclosed? (2) What use will be made of such information? Perhaps the order should be reversed, since disclosure requirements should be related to the use to be made of them.

There is some check on organizations which must replenish their funds from current donations, provided that putative donors are able to assess the quality of the job being done. Here enforced disclosure can play an informing role provided that the data supplied to government agencies is translated into understandable form and brought to donors' attention. Most present statutes and ordinances do not provide that soliciting charities must supply donors with facts, and creation of an analogue to the stock prospectus is quite difficult to accomplish.

Nevertheless, the data in government files may be studied by news reporters, executive officials, or by legislative committees, and any of these agencies may seek in an informal fashion to bring abuses to the attention of the public. The potential of such action can thus constitute a check, though it would be much more effective against the larger foundations, which are least likely to operate in an inefficient and ineffective manner. However, the airing of alleged abuses by public charges is itself a method subject to irresponsible use, and likely to be helpful only in the more serious cases. This is not to suggest that governmentally enforced disclosure is undesirable. It may not enable government officials to supervise and thus improve the work of bona fide organizations, but it may help those organizations to improve themselves.

One might hope that enforced disclosure will over a period of time affect the thinking of the administrators and other personnel within philanthropic organizations. The problem exists primarily in the small charities with few or no full time officials. Their difficulties lie not in an unwillingness to do an effective job, but in inadequate training or time. A governmentally imposed requirement of qualified officials might be justified, though it does not seem to be immediately foreseeable. In any event, what is needed is a substitute for the competitive market mechanism—namely, the development of commonly understood and accepted standards of conduct, plus a willingness to engage in responsible and informed criticism of the actions of sister charities. Such standards need not have the specificity required for fair and effective governmental regulation, though they must eventually evolve into a tradition akin to the ethics of a profession.

Such a hope or expectation may merely reflect the counsel of innocence. On the other hand, it may constitute a realistic appraisal of the situation. Whether or not philanthropy is, as suggested here, an essential part of a free society, it is with us to stay for a long time. Its deficiencies of operation are not readily cured by direct government regulation. Surely, an effort is in order on the part of those within the field, led by the larger organizations, to encourage the development of a professional tradition.

WEALTH AND CULTURE *

by Eduard C. Lindeman

FOUNDATIONS OR funds have, of course, existed over a long period of history. Indeed, the notion itself seems to have first

* Wealth And Culture (New York; Harcourt, Brace, 1936), pp. 8-9, 11-12, 19-20, 44, 46. Eduard C. Lindeman was a social worker and long-time professor of social philosophy and social education at the New York School of Social Work, Columbia University.

occurred to the Middle Romans. But in no other civilization have such instruments been utilized so widely as in the United States. It may even be said that the foundation had become the ascendant American device for disposing of large accumulations of surplus wealth, although private bequests through testaments or wills still remain the traditional method for the mass of the population.

The rise and development of foundations reflect with unusual accuracy one phase of economic evolution. The characteristic American economy was one of production and not distribution; its basic principle was individual profits to the individual enterpriser. Under such a system, in which the major object of attention is production, it might be expected that surplus profits would sooner or later outrun the necessities of reinvestment. Accumulations of unexpended and unneeded wealth would inevitably arise. Where such balances come into existence the question of their disposition becomes acute. The possessors may, and usually do, spend considerable amounts on what Veblen so aptly called conspicuous consumption. Instead of owning one house they may own two, three, or five, and each in a different location. Apologetic economists have often argued on the side of such expenditures, insisting that the luxuries of the rich implied employment for the poor. To live luxuriously, so the argument ran, represents one method for redistributing wealth. But it is, nevertheless, a non-economic distribution of wealth insofar as it does not tend to elevate the standard of living nor the security of the entire wealth-producing population. Another channel for accumulated wealth which is not needed in productive enterprise is provided by speculation. The consequence of increased speculation is to increase the ostensible value of securities. Superficially, this process appears to produce prosperity; industries whose stocks are selling "high" tend to expand and often increase wages and salaries. However, the major distribution of wealth (in this instance, largely fictitious) is on behalf of the security-holders, that is, the speculators. Ultimately, this procedure, when not accompanied by widespread increase in wages and reduction in prices, becomes a boomerang, and results in periodic depressions and economic crises.

In view of the unsatisfactory nature of the two above modes for disposing of surplus wealth it is not surprising that a third and more "worthy" method should have come into existence. If surplus money cannot be spent entirely on luxuries, and if increased speculations result in cyclical depressions, there is still the remaining outlet of philanthropy. At this point foundations arise. The distinction between ordinary private charity and large-scaled philanthropy is the difference between a small and a large surplus. The former may remain on a personal level but the latter involves organization. . . .

It is my assumption that the major influences in shaping the quality of American life during the decade here under consideration (1921–1930) may be listed in the following order of importance:

1. Business, commerce, industry, and finance
2. The Press
3. Schools, colleges, universities, and technological institutes
4. Churches and religious institutions
5. Governmental agencies
6. Foundations
7. Sports and amusements
8. Secret societies
9. Literature
10. The Fine Arts

It is not feasible to support an opinion of this sort with demonstrable data. By "quality of American life" I mean the ends, goals, values, for which Americans as a whole have striven. It seems to me clear that these cultural values have been influenced primarily by pecuniary and technological considerations; that knowledge, reasoning, justice, and beauty have been interpreted largely in terms of their relationship to material acquisitiveness and personal competitiveness. It also seems clear to me that all agencies of cultural influence must ultimately be appraised with respect to their contributions on behalf of, or in opposition to, this value-system. For present purposes it is not important to designate any special order of influence but merely to indicate that in our civilization vested wealth has come to be one of the primary instruments for determining cultural values. That this is the case seems to me incontrovertibly true. Foundations have, during this decade, influenced directly and indirectly all of the institutions which condition human behavior. Only two significant exceptions need to be made, namely, on behalf of the Press and Government. But, even here there are indications of both direct and indirect influence. Foundations have subsidized journals of various sorts, particularly of a technical and semi-technical character, and even researches conducted under the auspices of governmental agencies and persons have been financed by funds from foundations.

The peculiar nature of foundation influence is to be found, not primarily in the size of pecuniary contributions to various enterprises, but rather in the fact that foundation contributions represent that essential supplement to public and private [individual] funds which spells success or failure. In other words, foundations do not represent a "conspiracy" on the

78

part of the guardians of vested wealth designed to influence culture in one direction. More accurate would be the statement that these vested funds represent a consistently conservative element in our civilization, and that wherever their appropriations are accepted there enters at the same time this subtle influence in the direction of protecting the value system in existence, that is, of conserving the status quo. . . . In the midst of a cultural crisis it becomes relevant to ask those who purposefully influence cultural developments how they arrive at choices, preferments, and values. This question is especially apposite with respect to foundations, not merely because they make a direct impact upon culture, but because of their vastly more important indirect influence. Foundations do not merely exercise power and control over those who accept their money. Such influence is obvious even when the foundations making grants insist to the contrary. A more subtle and much more widespread control comes about by reason of the multitude of indirect relationships in which foundations play a part. Those who accept foundation grants often turn out to be radical critics, in private, of the control which has been exercised over them and their programs. Those who live in anticipation of receiving foundation grants are the more servile. Another device for projecting foundation control has become popular in recent years: foundations frequently supply the initial funds for a new project, these funds to be used for exploratory and conferencing purposes. In many cases the foundation acts as host for such preparatory groups. By the time the final project is formulated it becomes clear that nothing will be proposed or performed which may be interpreted as a challenge to the orthodox conception of value which characterizes foundations as a whole. Very few important cultural projects

79

of any size are consummated in this country without having experienced either the direct or indirect impact of foundation philosophy and influence. . . .

With such facts before us it becomes relatively simple to derive an adequate picturization of the type of individual who makes the decisions, influences the policies and purposes, and determines where the money vested in foundations is to go. Approximations of this sort do not, of course, furnish an adequate graph of any single individual trustee but they do allow us to describe the group as a whole from which foundation trustees are selected. With this limitation in mind, it seems fair to state that a typical trustee of an American foundation is a man well past middle age; he is more often than not a man of considerable affluence, or one whose economic security ranks high; his social position in the community is that of a person who belongs to the higher income-receiving class of the population; he is, presumably, "respectable" and "conventional" and belongs to the "best" clubs and churches, and he associates with men of prestige, power, and affluence. His training has been largely in the arts and humanities and he possesses only a slight background in the sciences, and technologies. He resides in the Northeastern section of the United States and has attended one of the private colleges in that region. His "intelligence" is ranked high by various institutions of higher learning from whom he has received signal honors. He receives his income primarily from profits and fees. In short, he is a member of that successful and conservative class which came into prominence during the latter part of the nineteenth and early twentieth century, the class whose status is based primarily upon pecuniary success.

SUPPORT FOR SOCIAL RESEARCH *

by Donald Young

IN THE American tradition foundations, like institutions of higher learning, welfare agencies, and other benevolent organizations, are administered by trustees and officers who, with few but notable exceptions, can only be described as amateurs in the accomplishment of the objectives of such organizations. Foundations of course have problems of management involving matters of law, investment, or public relations which make it highly desirable that these fields be represented on the board of directors. It is taken for granted that directors with these skills will participate fully in the consideration of all proposals. They must nevertheless be regarded as amateurs, albeit amateurs of integrity and good judgment; when decisions must be made on technical matters of health, welfare, education, or research, and need the aid of colleagues proficient in their foundations' areas of operation.

Primary dependence of foundations on trustees who are public-spirited citizens of good ability and repute has assured high purpose and a generally high level of managerial integrity. It is a pattern of management which worked especially well in the less complex days when it was established, and still can work well when a foundation operates in a relatively

* "Support for Social Research," *Foundation News,* 4 (January, 1963), 1–3. Donald Young is a sociologist and former foundation executive. From 1955–1963 he served as President of the Russell Sage Foundation. In 1964 he was appointed a visiting professor at the Rockefeller Institute in New York City.

81

small community or has a comparatively simple task, such as the distribution of its income to well-known agencies for their established programs. On the other hand, the disregard of many modern broad-purpose foundations operating in our involved urban society for specificity in trustee knowledge and experience has permitted the development and persistence of excessive anti-intellectualism in concern with social affairs, dependence on superficial information in decision making, and self-imposed isolation in operation. Note that it is said that these traits are excessively prevalent, not that they are all-pervading.

Anti-intellectualism may be thought too strong a term to use in referring to foundations' general practice of plunging ahead with projects and programs of social amelioration with little or no regard for preparatory research or later evaluative review. Certainly their major emphasis on education and on research in the physical and biological sciences is evidence that they are strongly pro-academic in matters concerning the material world and life itself. In contrast, attack on the problems of social living, of people getting along together in communities, in nations, and in a world made up of troubled nations, commonly is thought to require action without the delay and expense incident to rigorous study. Also, it is humanly more interesting and rewarding to deal directly with people's woes than to study their origin and nature in the hope that the resulting knowledge will lead to improved ameliorative and preventive measures.

Acceptance by foundation managers of the popular view that social questions are best answered by common sense and a warm heart encourages dependence for proposals, and advice in decision making, on like-minded individuals. Friendship and compatible bias afford personal reassurance in deciding whose advice to seek and what proposal to support when adequate technical knowledge is lacking. Furthermore, it is far from easy for the layman to obtain dependable advice on the relative utility—for his purposes—of the various social disciplines, or on the comparative merits of individual social scientists. There is common confusion concerning the relative advantages and limitations of sociology, social psychology, social anthropology, geography, political science, and economics for improved understanding of a given social problem. The distinction between social research and social practice also is rarely clear; there have been and will continue to be many foundation grants for social research to be carried out by social workers and psychiatrists with training and experience primarily in practice.

Western culture's respect for individual privacy limits receptivity to the research approach in human affairs. The intimate story of an individual's life and troubles is conceded to be pretty much his own affair, if no law is broken, and preferably kept to himself unless he is a public figure. The notion persists that, ideally, social problems are best solved by those who have them and next best by kindly relatives and neighbors or volunteer citizens. In other words, although concern for individual welfare is a social virtue, action growing out of such concern should in the minds of many avoid the appearance of an invasion of privacy—a difficult accomplishment if social research is to be utilized.

Philanthropy, too, is a private matter in the American ethos. True, the legal privilege accorded foundations of escaping the two allegedly inescapable eventualities, death and taxes, assumes acceptance of the principle that as public trusts they are subject to the requirement of ultimate public accountability. Nevertheless, the tradition of attributing special

83

virtue to privacy in benevolence, and the concept of individual freedom in disposal of private property, have helped keep social research a minor factor in foundation social benefactions. Emphasis on privacy argues against the use of social science analysis in foundation programs and projects, and imposes no need for evaluation of accomplishment. Furthermore, the socially approved desire for privacy perhaps has been the dominant factor in the persistence of a policy of isolation of foundations from each other in operation. This policy of not learning from each other's experience is defended as a means for assuring independent objective appraisals of proposals so that one rejection may not lead to others; to the extent that it is valid at all, the argument is a confession of weakness. The socially granted privilege of giving for the benefit of others through the instrumentality of a foundation carries with it the obligation to give wisely on the basis of a full knowledge of relevant circumstances and modern investigative techniques, a principle incompatible with secrecy and isolation in foundation giving.

Foundations avoid controversy like the plague. Granted that no one seeks criticism and attack in the performance of an intended good deed, there is reason to fear public disapproval of support for social research and action in areas of strong citizen sentiment. Fundamental in this avoidance pattern is the understandably prevailing attitude that social stability is good and that the burden of proof is on those who urge that some modification of existing patterns and values is desirable or even worthy of consideration. This is a sharp challenge to those who consider foundation funds "venture capital" or "risk money." In fact, proportionately very little foundation money is expended as "risk money." The bulk is invested in "blue chip" agencies and projects where there is little chance of public controversy and criticism, very nearly as it would be invested if expended directly by those who made or inherited it.

The fact that all but a small fraction of foundation grants are made to well-established agencies, and for relatively standard activities likely to be well received by press, legislature, and the general public is not mentioned here as criticism. In so expending their funds foundations are serving the main function for which they have been granted privileged status by society. It is an important function—if only because the resulting diversity of support and direction of scientific, educational, and charitable efforts is needed to help avoid stultifying homogeneity in management and operation. And, continuously, there is a small but significant stream of foundation money flowing into venturesome projects in controversial areas. Those who regret that this stream is not much larger may ask themselves how much it might be increased before social disapproval were to bring about restrictive action.

The foundations must inevitably expand their activity in social research, training, and application, in consequence of the path-breaking example set by the federal government. It has long been said that foundations have the advantage of freedom to pioneer with projects far too controversial or uncertain of results for support by tax money under political control. This has been important in the past and may be important again in the future, but does not seem so at present. Foundations have yielded leadership in such controversial areas as race relations, medical care, care of the economically and socially disadvantaged, prevention of unemployment and poverty, mental health, and others. In the physical and biological sciences the government is taking as great risks as any foundation ever did. In the social sciences the federal government is far in advance of the foundations in basic research, training, and application, not just in the number of dollars expended but, more importantly, also in dependence on professional peers of applicants in the selection of projects, institutions, and individuals for support, in the breadth of subject matter and method accepted for consideration, and in willingness to accept the fact that many projects must fail in order that the unpredictable one of significance may not be missed.

A CRITIQUE OF
AMERICAN FOUNDATIONS *

by Burton Raffel

THE PRINCIPLE of the private foundation is, I believe, inherently good. I do not in the least join with the disestablishmentarians. I want foundations to be better—always better, continually better. I also believe they need to be better, good as they are. Their social utility depends, ultimately, on their ability to be better: it is not enough to be good.

My main concern is that foundations are not living up to their potential, that their role as an impetus toward innovation is not being fulfilled as it could and should be. Despite all the talk of "seed money," it tends to be the safe bets on which foundations have been relying, of late. Our society not only has a place for an unrestricted, uninstitutionalized moiety of

* "A Critique of American Foundations," *Foundation News*, 4 (May, 1965), 45–48. Burton Raffel is a former editor of *Foundation News* and teaches English at the State University of New York at Stony Brook.

investment capital—which is what, after all, a foundation is—
but it has a positive need for such capital. The theory is
noble; the practice is tending to be conservative, cautious, and
distinctly non-innovational.

Let me begin with the selection and use of trustees. Foundations are funded organizations; they do not need, for economic reasons, a board composed of an impressive collection
of titles and status-names. Foundation trustees should be men
of ideas, should be specifically selected for the sake of their
ideas. They should not be figureheads, they should not be fa-
mous but frantically busy men with so many prior commitments that even attendance at trustee meetings is a difficult
chore. They should not be overage—though it is, I realize,
possible to be overage at thirty or young at eighty. They
ought to be men of concern, of dedication, men who would
like to see social motion and who are prepared to devote
themselves toward assisting it.

These are generalities: most of those who pick foundation
trustees, today, would probably agree with most such broad
requirements. But most of those who pick trustees, today, are
themselves trustees—a poor system, a self-perpetuation device
which sharply militates against exactly that impetus toward
change which is needed. Some continuity is of course desirable; some braking against over-hasty change is also important. But the current system provides much too much continuity and braking action. I suggest that no more than one-half
of the votes which select new trustees should be cast by those
who are already trustees. A ten-member board might for example coopt, at election time, ten outside electors—and not
exclusively institutional outsiders. The community foundations unfortunately tend toward such exclusively institutional
outside electors: the judge of this court, the head of that of-

fice. I should like to see a foundation concerned with medicine choose young doctors as electors; a foundation concerned with community planning choose young architects; a foundation concerned with the arts choose young artists, young writers. I would further suggest that these outside electors—whose function, I repeat, would be only to help choose new trustees—should serve for no more than say ten years, and should then name their own successors. The idea is to ensure the selection of men—and women—with reasonably fresh ideas, not bound by too many pre-existing limitations of social, professional, or institutional commitment. Permitting these electors no more than a decade of service would serve to block a new growth of ingrown tendencies. (I would like to see a similar time limitation on service as a foundation trustee.) And who could better choose men of the same fresh, independent cast of mind than could these electors?

But yet another reason for vitalizing foundation boards is the fact that foundation staff too have unfortunate tendencies which need to be resisted. Staff are too often arrogant, overly secure in the doling out of that universally welcome commodity, money. A truly active board can act as a corrective to this sort of thing. And the contrary disease in staff, timidity, is curable by precisely the same remedy. Staff which knows what trustees think, how they think, which has had the advantage of actually evolving programs with trustees, can act with far more decisiveness, and with much less fear of being overruled. It is the old story: health and vigor at the top quickly percolate downward. I have heard staff people talk in terms of seducing trustees into a knowledge of foundation programs and problems; I have heard staff people talk in terms of circumventing trustees, or, contrariwise, of being obliged to cotton to unfortunate, outdated approaches. But an honest staff-trustee partnership is really not so difficult an ideal to realize, given the kind of preparation I have been suggesting.

I have not been talking, plainly, about vest-pocket foundations, run from somebody's desk (often the donor's), with rubber-stamp trustees, no staff, and all too often with considerable and misapplied assets. Any foundation with a million dollars of capital can afford a part-time professional staff member; all foundations of whatever size should have access to some sort of professional staff assistance. An organization —or several organizations—like the Kansas City Association of Trusts and Foundations should exist in every city and region where foundations exist. Too much vest-pocket foundation giving is fumbling, uncertain, even wasted, because there is no sense of larger purposes and realities, even no awareness of simple facts—exactly the qualities and the data which professional staff can provide.

Foundation theory—which as I have said does not always correspond with the facts—prescribes that one gives to people, not to projects. I have in effect followed the theory, thus far, because foundations, like all institutions, only exist insofar as men make them exist. But foundations of course do not exist *in vacuo*. They give grants to other institutions, and to a lesser extent to individuals; they coexist with, and frequently depend upon other institutions, and to a lesser extent on individuals. Foundation dependence is a matter of administration; foundation giving is a matter of program.

If someone had asked a well-informed American, in the year 1900, what was (or where was) the center of intellectual strength in this country, the answer would probably have been "in the learned professions." No geographical or institutional locus would have been mentioned, though a passing nod might well have been given to Harvard or to Johns Hopkins. But the answer would be very different today: "in the universities," the same well-informed American would necessarily and correctly reply. The effect on foundation administration and programs of this enormous expansion in the number, the strength, and the status of our colleges and universities, has been extraordinary. Foundation staff tend to come from university posts (the list of earned PhD's alongside the names of The Rockefeller Foundation staff is illustrative). Foundation programs tend either to be administered by, or at the least framed with the active advice and cooperation of universities. The Ford Foundation is preparing a program in literary translation: the foundation has announced, surprising no one, that it will put that program into the hands of academics, and will locate it at a university. Carnegie Corporation of New York has always been deeply concerned with education, but the list of 17 new grants, in a recent *Quarterly*, includes 15 grants to universities, and one to a scholarly library for the use of college students. Grant applications to such organizations as The American Philosophical Society and John Simon Guggenheim Memorial Foundation, both of which give to individuals rather than to institutions, are reviewed and in essence decided upon by committees largely composed of academics. American Philosophical Society grants are awarded largely to academics—and the Guggenheim Foundation's most recent grants, those for 1964–65, went 90 per cent to academics, a pattern this foundation has maintained for some years, and a general tendency it has been displaying for several decades.

There is nothing wrong with taking intellectual support from the centers of intellectual strength, nor with giving support to these same centers. The difficulty, as I see it, is that foundations have come to be overly dependent on universities, both in administration (i.e., advice, counsel, planning) and in program (i.e., the giving of money). Recently, The Ford Foundation wanted information about the state of American humanistic learning, in a variety of disciplines. To whom did it turn, in its study of academe? To American academics: the study was therefore a self-study. There is, again, nothing wrong with self-study; psychiatrists frequently recommend it. But one must be sharply aware of the fact that self-study is that and no more, that self-study is by its nature limited, that it is by its nature less than fully objective. I have seen no signs of this awareness, in connection with Ford's multi-volumed study of humanistic studies. Another large foundation was approached by someone doing pioneering and distinctly scholarly work in an area with which the foundation is much concerned; the grant was not made, simply because the applicant was not an academic. And one intensely practical sign that the universities are well aware of the situation is the mushrooming of "foundation specialists" on campus after campus.

There are obvious dangers for the universities themselves, in this excessively symbiotic situation. Faculty members come to have a distaste for teaching, when obtaining funds for research is relatively so easy; university administrative costs increase, without fiscal recompense; universities and their faculties find themselves involved in projects simply because the money is offered, money being notoriously difficult to turn down. But my emphasis, here, is on the foundations—and I think the dangers for them are equally clear. Foundations are not so necessary to universities, by now, as universities are to foundations. Foundation money is an attractive but not a massive part of university budgets; they have survived without such sources of funds before, and could do so again. But to whom would the foundations turn, in administration and in program, if the universities were not there? Foundation dependence has reached the point where the question would seem, to many trustees and staff persons, unanswerable. But what did foundations do before the universities reached their present eminence? Some of them ran their own programs, as Russell Sage and Twentieth Century Fund still do, programs which often run parallel to certain university developments, but which by the very fact of being independent are able to achieve different and useful results. Some foundations established institutes and research centers, a pattern Ford tried and, I think mistakenly, has largely abandoned. Both these methods may, and usually will, employ university-trained people—but there is a large and healthy distinction between a campus scholar and one out in the great world. The contrast improves all parties—the world, the foundation, and the campus to which the scholar may eventually return. In those early days, too, foundations were a good deal more like "action organizations" than they are today—and unlike the Internal Revenue Service I define an "action organization" as one which acts, whether in strengthening usury laws or in eradicating yellow fever. That is, then as now foundations were conduits, directing funds into useful channels, but they did not then so often employ brokers to hire and direct the work for them. They were *involved*, they were themselves committed, *engagé*. Even Gunnar Myrdal's classic study of the American Negro, a scholarly study if ever there was one (and based, too, on technical scholarship of the most rigorous kind), even that study was conducted between Carnegie Corporation and Myrdal, not between Carnegie and a university. There is an enormously important difference in these two methods of procedure. Nor is it an accident, I think, that

Myrdal's book (*An American Dilemma*), and many written under similar circumstances, are superior to most work being written under foundation sponsorship today. The advantage of the independently organized study lies, I think, principally in flexibility, in recognition that a university post does not per se make a man objective and talented, and even in an awareness that university posts sometimes exercise the opposite effect (in part because of the deadening effect of most graduate education, in part because of the institutional formalisms and internal politics of universities).

The Ford Foundation—which excels in both the good and the bad—has given some continuing recognition to these principles. Ford's grants to non-academics, e.g., for the type of studies and self-education projects which only academics usually are able to work at, are a healthy step. But a very small step—and Ford seems to me excessively influenced by a principle closely associated with the notion of university omnipotence. I call it the "Lincoln Center" complex, i.e., the terribly mistaken notion that commercially successful art and architecture and what-have-you is the pinnacle of achievement; commercial success is thus the analogue of PhD and a professorship. Many other foundations share this notion—and though all parties stoutly deny that foundation grants are stamps of approval, rewards to the successful for their success, how else explain the kinds of people to whom foundation moneys now go?

There is yet another explanation, to be sure, for the timidity—and it is that—which requires such heavily authenticated credentials before it will venture to invest a bit of seed money. Foundations have been more venturesome in the past, yes, and they have gotten, in return, a series of more or less infamous congressional investigations. The traumata are terribly distinct; the scars are difficult of healing, when so many wounds are every day being opened and reopened. And yet it does not seem to me that cowering and institutional timidity are the proper answer to make to these critics. Foundations achieved a great deal more, by their earlier pioneering, than the enmity of the loud and know-nothing wings of American politics (and know-nothings we will have always with us, in any event). Foundations earned the reputation for profound accomplishment, for humanitarianism, for intelligence and flexibility and speed of action. One of the victims of the Nazis left a bequest to The Rockefeller Foundation: is anyone likely to have such a warm feeling for the same foundation, today, or for Carnegie, or Ford, or Sloan, or Kellogg, or the Duke Endowment, or the Pew Memorial Trust?

Part Three
Propaganda and Politics

FOUNDATIONS: THEIR
POWER AND INFLUENCE *

by René A. Wormser

OVER THE past few decades the major foundation complex has operated almost as an informal but integral arm of government, acting, to a very considerable extent, as its collateral "brain trust," and determining policy. If a revolution has indeed been accomplished in the United States, we can look here for its motivation, its impetus, and its rationale.

Communist Penetration of Foundations

A good part of the impetus of the "revolution" came from Marxists. To what extent some of it came from actual Communists, we shall probably never be able to piece together adequately—but there can be equally little doubt that much of it was Communist-inspired. The presence of so many disclosed Communists in government during the New Deal and Fair Deal eras makes this conclusion inevitable. There is, moreover, much evidence that Communists made substantial, direct inroads into the foundation world, using its resources to promote their ideology.

* From *Foundations: Their Power and Influence* (New York: Devin-Adair, 1958), pp. 174–175, 178–181, 196–199, and 200–206. René Wormser has been a practicing attorney in New York since 1920 and is an authority on estate planning. In 1953 he was appointed General Counsel for the Reece Committee, and his volume on foundations reflects the conclusions reached in the Reece Committee's majority report.

The Reece Committee has been castigated for asserting that subversive influences have played a part in the history of foundations in the United States. Yet it was its predecessor, the Cox Committee, which made this utterly plain, in so far as actual Communist penetration of foundations was concerned. That Committee produced evidence which supported its conclusion that there had been a Moscow-directed, specific plot to penetrate the American foundations and to use their funds for Communist propaganda and Communist influence upon our society. There was also evidence that this plot had succeeded in some measure.

We shall never know the full extent of this penetration, but testimony before the Cox Committee disclosed that The Marshall Field Foundation, The Garland Fund, The John Simon Guggenheim Foundation, The Robert Marshall Foundation, The Rosenwald Foundation, and The Phelps Stokes Fund had been successfully penetrated or used by Communists. The Marshall and Garland foundations had, in fact, lost their tax exemptions. The Cox investigation also disclosed that almost a hundred discovered grants to individuals and organizations with extreme leftist records or affiliations had been made by some of the more important foundations, including The Rockefeller Foundation, The Carnegie Corporation, The Carnegie Endowment for International Peace, The John Simon Guggenheim Foundation, The Russell Sage Foundation, The William C. Whitney Foundation and The Marshall Field Foundation. . . .

The mandates of both the Cox and Reece Committees went further than a mere exploration of "subversion." The Cox Committee was to inquire into activities which were not in the "interests or tradition of the United States"; the Reece Committee, into the support of "un-American activities."

These terms are almost impossible to define with complete certainty. They can only be related to *a priori* standards of value, standards which cannot be arrived at through an empirical approach. There are conflicting ways in which historical facts can be interpreted to prove what the tradition of the United States may be. One can make a case for the claim that various types of sectarian socialism are traditionally characteristic of parts of our farm population. One can submit "proof" in the form of data about continued devotion to ideas originally promoted by early religious community settlements, and their survival in various forms of Federal farm support and soilbanking schemes. However, there was sufficient general clarity in the mandates of the two Committees for inquiry purposes. Socialism is basically antithetical to our system.

All Socialists do not recognize themselves as such. But it is, after all, their private affair. They are entitled to be Socialists if they care to, whether or not they are aware that socialism cannot exist without force and oppression, that it must otherwise fail for economic reasons. In a democracy, the citizen has the right to his reasonable mistakes, disastrous as they may be to the public welfare. The free contest of ideas would usually save us from such evils as doctrinaire socialism. But, in our country, the free market for ideas has rapidly declined. The one-sided support by foundations of the utopian Socialists has created a constricted and limited market place.

So the real problem which faced the two recent investigations was the imbalance in the struggle of ideas, created by the preference of foundation giving in the two decades from 1930 to 1950. The virulent criticism to which Congressional investigation of foundations has been subjected has perverted an investigation of this imbalance into an alleged attack on civil liberties.

The true problem is not whether Socialists or extreme "liberals" are respectable and entitled to their views but rather that their opponents have been discriminated against in the allotment of funds by major foundations. The ascendancy of Socialistic ideas is attributable, partly at least, to this foundation-created imbalance.

The Reece Committee did not disparage liberalism. It said: "We cannot too strongly state that this Committee respects the true liberal and deems him as important to the proper political functioning of our society as is the conservative." It did attack the kind of person who calls himself a "liberal" but is not. Such a "liberal," said the Committee, "travels *IN* if not *UNDER* the same direction" as communism—he may even be "a violent and inveterate opponent of communism," but he gives it support by falling into "the error of wishing to destroy before he knows the significance of that with which he wishes to replace."

And so, continued the Committee, the foundations have frequently been persuaded by these ardent men-in-a-hurry to use trust funds for "risk capital," without fairly measuring the social risk.

This "risk capital" concept, which has found such wide favor among major foundation executives, propels them "into a constant search for something new, a pathological scrutinizing of what we have, on the premise that there must be something better." There is much room for improvement in our society, but much of what we have is considered by the great majority of Americans sound and inviolate. The pathological "liberal" propulsion into taking social risks seems invariably to skip the study of what we have that is good and should be preserved; instead, it supports change for change's sake, or on the general theory that the different thing *must* be better.[1] Much of this "risk taking" assists communism.

That Socialistic ideas can be legally promoted in the United States, that prominent figures have openly adopted them in the disguise of "reform," does not make them any less "subversive." If one accepts the concepts and principles of the Declaration of Independence and the Constitution as expressions of the existing order, then any attempt to replace them with the concepts and principles of socialism must be considered "subversive" and "un-American." Moreover, there is continued danger that the Communist who has recently been converted over to what might be called simple socialism may switch back again in his allegiance. Many of the intellectuals who departed from Communism did so because they disagreed with Stalin; some of these will still support communism of a variety differing only slightly from the old orthodoxy. . . .

Leftists Supplied to Government by Foundations

It is an understatement to say that the majority of the Reece Committee was shocked at Professor Kenneth Colegrove's revelations concerning the extent to which foundation-supported organizations had been responsible for the penetration of Communists and Communist sympathizers into the government as advisers.

When advisers were to be selected in social-science areas for our occupation authorities in Germany and Japan, Professor Colegrove submitted, as Secretary of The American Political Science Association, upon request of the government, a list of proposed political advisers. While he himself was appointed

[1] Reece Committee *Report*, pp. 201–202.

and took office as an adviser to General MacArthur (not at his own suggestion), his list was completely ignored. He found, to his dismay, that the advisers had been selected entirely from lists supplied by two other organizations. One was the notorious Institute of Pacific Relations, so generously supported by The Rockefeller Foundation, The Carnegie Corporation, and The Carnegie Endowment for International Peace. The other was The American Council of Learned Societies, another intermediary organization heavily supported by major foundations.

The Communist connections of IPR have been mentioned. In the case of The American Council of Learned Societies, its Executive Secretary was Dr. Mortimer Graves, whose list of Communist-front associations impressed even the Cox Committee. Here we have two of the executive agencies of what the Reece Committee report called the "concentration of power" or the complex supported by some of the major foundations.

Professor Colegrove checked the list of accepted appointees. He testified as follows:

We checked these names off. Some of them were known to us to be Communists, many of them pro-Communists or fellow travelers. They were extremely leftist.

I went back to the Pentagon to protest against a number of these people, and to my amazement I found that they had all been invited, and they had all accepted, and some of them were already on their way to Japan.[2]

The committee report had this to say about Dr. Graves:

We do not accuse Mr. Graves of being a Communist. But it amazes us that one with so evident a lack of political and social

[2] *Ibid.*, p. 201.

discernment, with such apparent lack of objectivity, should be retained as a directing officer in what purports to be the representative organization for all the social sciences and humanities. Mr. Graves still holds his position, though the Cox Committee hearings brought out his extensive record of Communist-front affiliations. This leads us to conclude one of two things; either his personal power is astounding or the extreme political slant of an executive is deemed of no moment by that tax-exempt agency of the foundations.[3]

In writing the platform for the Communist League, Marx and Engels predicted that the proletariat would "use its political supremacy to wrest, by degrees, all capital from the bourgeoisie, to centralize all instruments of production in the hand of the state, i.e., of the proletariat organized as a ruling class." A considerable number of the planks of the Communist Manifesto have become part of the law of our land; but this has been accomplished not through a seizure of power by a "proletariat" but through the misguided efforts of our intellectuals. Most of these intellectuals lead a life remote from the economic realities of society. Educators, in general, are among the most valuable of our citizens. But they usually do not know the market place; their ideas of how an economy should or can run are often as impractical as they are idealistic. True, they can sometimes support unrealistic theories with a mass of empirical data, but it is usually both incomplete and unsound because it excludes vital factors not susceptible to empirical study.

The undeniable fact is that the changes which have taken place in the United States were not the result of the "despotic inroads on the right of property, and on the conditions of bourgeois production." They were the result of continuous

[3] *Ibid.*, p. 55.

propaganda in the form of biased education. This propaganda has nearly convinced the American people that the Marxian formula is good for it.

The fog-bound intellectuals who have advocated change on the theory that things are not as rosy as they should be and, therefore, anything else would be better, have blindly permitted themselves to be led into the path of socialism. Whereas, today they generally despise communism, the intellectual proponents of change in America still consider socialism as eminently respectable. They still do not see the central identity of communism and other forms of socialism; they believe that a gradual transition of our society to one in which "production" is "for use and not for profits" can prevail without any suppression of freedom. The bloody extermination of liberty in Russia is, to these intellectuals, merely an evidence that the Stalinist variety of socialism is reprehensible. They are disappointed lovers, rather than true opponents. They are blind to this fact: whether the approach to socialism is by way of force or soft propaganda, the system will inevitably call for the rape of the masses, for the suppression of liberty and freedom.

The ideas of socialism have too long been supported in our country by fashions of thought which, in turn, have been heavily financed by foundations. Critics of foundation activity have wondered, indeed, why foundations have had so little interest in several obvious fields of "venturing." They might well "venture" heavily into studies of what is worth preserving in our system and in our society; into education that promotes traditions and established values; into public-affairs programs which promote national pride and national ambitions.

There is some hope. The foundations today seem to be slightly more cautious in supporting Socialist politics under the disguise of education and research than before the Congressional investigations took place. But caution is not enough. In addition to taking care to see that their funds are not used for anti-social purposes, it behooves them also to support constructive programs in the social sciences, in education and in public affairs. . . .

There is still hope that the trustees of some of those foundations which have acted as the financial underwriters of socialism in the United States may force a change in the ways of the organization whose cerebral management they have neglected. . . .

The Foundation Complex in "Internationalism"

Foundation activity has nowhere had a greater impact than in the field of foreign affairs. It has conquered public opinion and has largely established the international-political goals of our country. A few major foundations with internationalist tendencies created or fostered a varied group of organizations which now dominate the research, the education, and the supply of experts in the field. Among such instruments are the Council on Foreign Relations, the Foreign Policy Association, the Institute of Pacific Relations, the United Nations Association, and the conferences and seminars held by American universities on international relations and allied subjects.

It would be difficult to find a single foundation-supported organization of any substance which has not favored the United Nations or similar global schemes; fantastically heavy foreign aid at the burdensome expense of the taxpayer; meddling in the colonial affairs of other nations; and American military commitments over the globe. Though the sums of money put up by the internationalist-minded foundations may seem relatively small in comparison with larger grants spent elsewhere, they have enabled their satellite or subsidized organizations to play a conspicuous and dominating role. This was comparatively easy to accomplish because there was no organized or foundation-supported opposition.

The influence of the foundation complex in internationalism has reached far into government, into the policymaking circles of Congress and into the State Department. This has been effected through the pressure of public opinion, mobilized by the instruments of the foundations; through the promotion of foundation-favorites as teachers and experts in foreign affairs; through a domination of the learned journals in international affairs; through the frequent appointment of State Department officials to foundation jobs; and through the frequent appointment of foundation officials to State Department jobs.

At least one foreign foundation has had a strong influence on our foreign policy. The Rhodes Scholarship Fund of Great Britain, created to improve England's international public relations but not registered here as a foreign agent, has gained great influence in the United States for British ideas. It has accomplished this by annually selecting a choice group of promising young men for study in England. The usually Anglophile alumni of this system are to be found in eminent positions in legislation, administration, and education and in the ranks of American foundation officials. They form a patronage network of considerable importance. Dr. Frank Aydelotte in a book, *The Rhodes Trust, 1903–1953* published in 1956, reported: "The influence of this group on American educational practice and particularly on the rapidly increasing maturity and breadth of methods of instruction in American institutions of higher learning, has been immense." He continued: "The number of those going into government is constantly increasing."

Of a total of 1,372 American Rhodes scholars up to 1953, 431 held or hold positions in teaching and educational administration (among them, 31 college presidents); 113 held government positions; 70 held positions in press and radio; and 14 were executives in other foundations. Dr. Aydelotte remarks: "One indication of success of operation of the Rhodes Scholarships in America is the remarkable way in which they have inspired other foundations." He reports that the Guggenheim fellowships and the program of the Commonwealth Fund set up by Mr. Harkness and several similar programs were developed with the aid of officials of the Rhodes fund.

Dean Rusk, president of The Rockefeller Foundation, and several of the staff members of that foundation are Rhodes scholars. Mr. Henry Allen Moe, the director of the Guggenheim foundation, and O. C. Carmichael, former president of the Carnegie foundation, are Rhodes Scholars. Senator J. W. Fulbright, Congressmen C. R. Clason, R. Hale, and C. B. Albert, and 14 American State legislators are also Rhodes alumni. Among the many Rhodes scholars connected with our Department of State are these: Ambassador to the Netherlands S. K. Hornbeck (formerly Chief of Far Eastern Affairs in the Department); B. M. Hulle (former Chief of North European Affairs in the Department); W. Walter Butterworth (former Assistant Secretary of State for Eastern Affairs, U. S. Ambassador to Sweden, Deputy Chief U. S. Mission to London); Walter Gordon (U. S. Embassy in London, in charge of Economic Affairs with the rank of minister); and G. C. McGhee (Ambassador to Turkey). Before becoming president of The Rockefeller Foundation, Dean Rusk served as a deputy Under-secretary of State. Dr. Aydelotte reports that, in addition, 12 Rhodes scholars were attached to various intergovernmental agencies (ILO, UN, etc.).

It may not be merely coincidental to this subject that Cecil Rhodes, who created the Scholarships, and Andrew Carnegie were friends. The latter may have learned from the former the technique of accomplishing great effects with relatively modest means. Carnegie contributed but a small part of his wealth to The Carnegie Endowment for International Peace; yet this comparatively small unit grew to have gigantic influence on American foreign affairs.

Just as there have been interlocks and a "concentration of power" in education and in social-science research in domestic areas, there has been a similar combination in the field of foreign policy. The major components of the concentration in internationalism have been The Carnegie Corporation, The Carnegie Endowment for International Peace, The Rockefeller Foundation, and, recently, The Ford Foundation. I have mentioned some of their more important satellites. Then there are the "conferences."

One of the most important activities of the foundations and associated groups operating in the international field consists of promoting conference after conference and forum after forum for the discussion of international affairs. These would serve a useful purpose were it not for the fact that they are almost invariably made into platforms for the special points of view which these groups favor.

A common character of the meetings frequently held all over the country under the auspices of or in cooperation with the organs of the internationalist foundations is that they regularly present speakers favorable to the sentiments of these supporters. The speakers, almost invariably and *ad nauseam*, advocate aid for underdeveloped countries "with no strings attached"; distribution of American foreign aid through the United Nations rather than through American agencies; recognition of Communist China; membership for Communist China in the United Nations; American abandonment of atomic weapons without guarantees for similar disarmament by our enemy. Through their virtually monopolistic control of the market place for ideas in the area of international relations, these organizations exert an influence far beyond the weight of the general followers of "liberal" politics. Their opponents enjoy little or no financial support. Thus, the intensity of the "internationalist" campaign produces propaganda returns even among businessmen and groups which would ordinarily, without the blasting of such propaganda, be inclined to a more conservative point of view.

For example, the *National Review* of March 7, 1956, called attention to the fact that The U.S. Chamber of Commerce had been among the sponsors of a recent Midwest Residential Seminar on World Affairs, held near St. Louis. It was in strange company. Among the other supporting organizations were The American Labor Education Service, The American Association for the United Nations, The Social Science Foundation, The Institute of International Relations, The Carnegie Endowment for International Peace, The American Library Association, The Foreign Policy Association, and The American Foundation for Political Education. *The featured speaker at this seminar was John Carter Vincent, discharged from the State Department as a loyalty risk.*

The Part of the Carnegie Endowment

When Andrew Carnegie established The Carnegie Endowment for International Peace, he gave the managers of this fund a difficult task. How were they to go about promoting peace? They seem to have had no very clear idea until Dr. Nicholas Murray Butler, in whose hands Mr. Carnegie put the initial direction of the fund, got excited about the peril of the Allies in World War I and decided that the best way to establish peace was to help get the United States into the War. To this end he began to use the Endowment funds.

When the war was ended, that issue was gone. Support for the League of Nations gave the Endowment one new outlet for its energies and its funds, but more scope than this was needed for the propaganda machine which it had become. A fruitful guide for operations was found in Dr. Butler's personal shibboleth of "the international mind," a phrase to which he was devoted in speeches and writings.

The concept of "the international mind" had considerable value. Americans generally, in Dr. Butler's day, were not as well informed in international affairs as might be desirable; efforts to educate them were commendable enough. But Dr. Butler went further than a mere desire to give us a better international education. He seemed to have had an idea that if only Americans got more "international-minded" the cause of peace would be promoted. Perhaps this is an exaggeration, as I state it, but there is no question that Dr. Butler was somewhat possessed of the concept of "international-mindedness."

At any rate, a powerful propaganda machine came into being. Used objectively, it could have been of enormous service to the country. But, as is likely to be the case, it turned to advocacy. When you control a propaganda vehicle, it is tempting to use it to promote your own program.

The Reece Committee said of the Endowment's work:

An extremely powerful propaganda machine was created. It spent many millions of dollars in:

The production of masses of material for distribution;

The creation and support of large numbers of international policy clubs, and other local organizations at colleges and elsewhere;

The underwriting and dissemination of many books on various subjects, through the "International Mind Alcoves" and the "International Relations Clubs and Centers" which it organized all over the country;

The collaboration with agents of publicity, such as newspaper editors;

The preparation of material to be used in school text books, and cooperation with publishers of text books to incorporate this material;

The establishing of professorships at the colleges and the training and indoctrination of teachers;

The financing of lecturers and the importation of foreign lecturers and exchange professors;

The support of outside agencies touching the international field, such as the *Institute of International Education, the Foreign Policy Association, the American Association for the Advancement of Science, the American Council on Education, the American Council of Learned Societies, the American Historical Association, the American Association of International Conciliation, the Institute of Pacific Relations, the International Parliamentary Union* and others, and acting as mid-wife at the birth of some of them.[4]

The Carnegie Endowment was utterly frank in disclosing its propaganda function. It used terms frequently such as the "education of public opinion." This is not "public education," but *molding public opinion.* The Committee report indicated that one thing seemed "utterly clear: no private group should have the power or the right to decide what should be read and taught in our schools and colleges," yet this is what the Endowment sought to do in "educating public opinion."

[4] *Ibid.,* p. 171.

The influence of this foundation may be illustrated by the functions held by its former president, Alger Hiss. He was a trustee of The Woodrow Wilson Foundation, a director of the executive committee of the American Association for the United Nations, a director of the American Peace Society, a trustee of the World Peace Federation, and a director of the American Institute of Pacific Relations.

FREEDOM, EDUCATION, AND THE FUND *

by Robert M. Hutchins

THE FOUNDATIONS have been uncommonly vocal recently; they have also been uncommonly unanimous. I have been dealing with the foundations in one way or another for more than thirty years. They have always been distinguished by their lack of fellow feeling. They have scorned a project if it required the co-operation of another foundation. It is therefore one of the more absurd charges of the Reece Committee that the foundations were an intellectual cartel. The Reece Committee forced them to huddle together in self-defense. One more investigation and they might become a cartel.

* *Freedom, Education, and the Fund: Essays and Addresses, 1946–1956* (New York: Meridian, 1956), pp. 201–207. Robert M. Hutchins was Dean of the Yale Law School from 1927–1929, President of the University of Chicago from 1929–1951, an associate director of the Ford Foundation from 1951 until June 1, 1954, and since that time has been President of the Fund for the Republic. The Fund was the object of several pages of charges by the Reece Committee for its often controversial activities. The excerpt was originally part of a speech delivered in the presence of Congressman Reece.

The conduct of the majority, if it was the majority, of the Reece Committee was so scandalous that it outraged almost all the press and apparently even one of its own members. At any rate, Angier L. Goodwin of Massachusetts wrote a new kind of concurring opinion, one that disagreed with all the conclusions of the opinion with which it purported to concur. In the conduct of the hearings Mr. Reece added some new wrinkles to the distortions that we have become accustomed to in congressional investigations.

The foundations were elaborately attacked by the staff and by some witnesses of dubious standing. Then, pleading that Mr. Hays of Ohio would not let him conduct the hearings as they should be conducted, Mr. Reece adjourned them and informed the foundations that they could file written statements. Perhaps the most depressing fact about the report of the so-called majority of the Reece Committee is that Mr. Reece takes credit for relieving the foundations of what he calls the "embarrassment" of cross-examination. You might as well execute an innocent man without the embarrassment of a hearing. If you did, however, nobody would have the affrontery to claim that you had conformed to the principles of Anglo-American jurisprudence.

The most entertaining of the new wrinkles was that the majority of the Committee took a philosophical position. The Cambridge ladies, e. e. cummings said, lived in furnished souls; so Mr. Reece and Mr. Wolcott came bustling out in second-hand suits of anti-empiricism, supplied them by the sages of the staff. Mr. Reece and Mr. Wolcott were much against empiricism, which they associated with moral relativism, irreligion, the cultural lag and ultimately with subversion.

The Congressmen could not be bothered with history. They overlooked the fact that some of the most empirical empiricists in history, like Hume and Montaigne, were thoroughgoing tories. The Congressmen could not be bothered with consistency: for example, they went after the teachers' colleges for sponsoring empiricism and then after the Fund for the Advancement of Education for not sponsoring the teachers' colleges.

If a committee may charge a foundation with empiricism, why not charge a college with it, and if with empiricism why not also with Presbyterianism or Catholicism or any other philosophy, religion, or dogma that the committee does not care for? The grant of tax exemption may carry with it certain obligations, and those who accept it may by implication agree that they must perform certain services. But it has never been supposed that by taking tax exemption a college, university, church, or foundation, otherwise within the law, was liable to condemnation because of the philosophy that it held. If there is such liability, the way is open to the most flagrant violation of religious freedom and of freedom of speech and teaching.

The lesson the majority, if it is a majority, of the Reece Committee wants to teach the foundations is stated in words of crystalline clarity: "They should be very chary of promoting ideas, concepts and opinion-forming material which run counter to what the public currently wishes, approves and likes."

Here the Committee throws overboard the principle accepted by the Cox Committee that the justification of the foundations is that they supply risk or venture capital in the field of philanthropy. That is what they are for, to take chances, the Cox Committee said. The Reece Committee would confine them to what a public relations man, presumably by a series of careful polls, found that the public currently wished, approved, and liked. The way to be safe would be to attract no attention, arouse no discussion, create no controversy.

Even this would not be enough. All the things of which the Committee now complains were currently wished, approved, and liked at the time the foundations did them. To meet the test laid down by the Committee, therefore, a foundation would have to be able to foresee what would become unpopular by the time of an investigation.

But even this is not enough. The issue is not what the public will wish, approve, and like. There is no evidence, for example, that the American public dislikes empiricism. Quite the contrary, the public does not dislike empiricism: the Reece Committee does, or rather two members of it do, or perhaps just the staff of the Reece Committee does. Running a foundation on these terms becomes an extra-hazardous occupation fraught with dangers that test pilots and submarine explorers and others who are up against nothing worse than the laws of Nature do not encounter.

The Reece Committee achieved some of its gaudiest effects by the simple process of giving old words new definitions and then pinning the old words on the foundations. This is the way that empiricism becomes subversive. Subversion now means, the Committee says, a promotion of tendencies that may lead to results that the Committee will not like. Hence support of the New Deal could be subversion. Social engineering, planning, world government, the United Nations, William James, John Dewey, the American Friends Service Committee, Dr. Kinsey and reform are all subversive in the bright new lexicon of the Reece Committee. And of course all these things are socialistic, if not communistic, too.

At times one feels when reading the report that old scurrilous words will be redefined and applied to any expression of decent human feeling. So it was that a staff member found himself identifying certain Papal Encyclicals as communistic.

But the Reece report is said to be a majority report, and it will be referred to in the future as a majority report. Its appendix will be quoted as an authoritative collection of dangerous names. The only reason for the appendix is to enable some committee in the future to say of somebody that he was listed by the Reece Committee. This fact will then be greeted with hushed and incredulous awe by those to whom it is communicated.

All you have to do to qualify for the appendix is to favor world government or get mentioned by the *Daily Worker*. The principal charge against one distinguished professor is that he is quoted, apparently with approval, in a dissenting opinion in the Circuit Court of Appeals. A low of some sort is reached with the mention in the appendix of the name of George F. Kennan. He is accused of the following—and this is the total record—: a book of his was reviewed (we are not told whether favorably or unfavorably) in the *Daily People's World* and the *New World Review;* on May 9, 1950, the New York *Times* reported that he spoke on Communist China (what he said does not appear); and on May 28, 1950, the New York *Times* reported that he "attacked witchhunting of Communists." On the basis of such information Mr. Kennan will in the future be referred to as "cited by the Reece Committee."

The appendix of the Reece Committee's so-called majority report is an endless carnival of good clean fun—it is almost two hundred pages long; but I must pass on. I cannot regard the Reece Committee as having more than symbolic or symptomatic importance. Its wild and squalid presentation affords a picture of the state of our culture that is most depressing. Its aims and methods are another example of the exploitation of public concern about Communism and subversion to further political ambition and to work off political grudges.

We may as well state it plainly: the Reece investigation in its inception and execution was a fraud. Nobody in his right mind could suppose that the great accumulations of wealth left by our richest men were being intentionally used by their trustees to overthrow the institutions of this country. Hence the Reece Committee had to take another tack: the trustees were said to be so busy that they had to leave the foundations to officers who were often quite disreputable. Though this relieved the men of wealth and standing of the charge of being knaves, it did so only at the expense of charging them with being fools. Only fools could be so careless as to allow enormous sums entrusted to them for charitable purpose to be stolen away and lavished on the subversion of their country.

Congress may properly investigate the foundations and seek to arrive at general legislative policy concerning them. But the most important question to ask about any given foundation is whether it is one. Is it actually using its money for religious, charitable, educational, or scientific purposes? The First Amendment suggests that tax exemption should not be denied or revoked because the particular views of religion, education, or science held or promoted by the foundation are unpopular.

On the other hand, nothing in the Constitution requires that tax exemption must be accorded an organization, which though in outward form a foundation, is actually a tax dodge, or a public relations device, or a scheme to promote the personal interests of the donor. The test is public versus private purposes. The Government may properly inquire into this question, since the exemption is granted with a promise of performance. The appropriate forum for the determination of the question of performance would seem to be a court.

As Dr. Johnson used to say, we must clear our minds of cant. When we do, we see that in general the foundations have for many years been following the prescription laid down for them by the majority of the Reece Committee. This prescription is to try to avoid doing what is or may become unpopular. The failure of the foundations to be universally popular at all times is seldom caused by a spirit of reckless abandon or eager pioneering on their part. It is caused rather by the difficulties of predicting what will be popular or unpopular.

Who could have imagined that helping prospective teachers in Arkansas to get an education would have ever been regarded by anybody as exhibiting dangerous tendencies of mind? But when a foundation did this, it was criticized by teachers, businessmen, and newspapers in that State and was of course complained of by the Reece Committee. What would the Foundation have done in Arkansas if it had been possible to foresee the reactions that in fact occurred? I do not say that the grant would not have been made, but I would not bet on it; for the foundations have in varying degrees suppressed their ambition to provide risk capital in favor of a desire to have what are called good public relations, that is, to avoid unpopularity.

We know that the Attorney-General's list is an *ex parte* finding of guilt with no probative standing in law. But how many foundations would give money to an organization or even to an individual in an organization on the Attorney-General's list, however meritorious the project? Would we support organizations that allowed groups listed by the Attorney-General to meet in halls owned by them? If not, for an irrelevant reason, one that has nothing to do with the quality of the proposal, but that has a great deal to do with our popularity, we have made our peace with Reece.

We know that the most dreadful aspect of the current situation is the atmosphere of suspicion and of guilt-by-association in which we live. We ought to say that until a man or an organization has been condemned by due process of law he or it must be presumed innocent, and therefore individuals and organizations are not to be automatically denied support solely on the ground that they are associated with unpopular people. Yet how many foundations would give money for a good purpose to be well carried out by an organization which, though not on the Attorney-General's list, was supposed to have some Communist members or was vaguely reported to be dominated by Communists?

We have come a long way since Lord Macaulay, who said, "To punish a man because we infer from some doctrine he holds or from the conduct of others who hold the same doctrine with him that he will commit a crime is persecution and is in any case foolish and wicked."

Congressman Reece was scoffed at. It was agreed that his investigation was a farce. I think he had good reason to be satisfied with himself. I think he won. Without firing a single serious shot, without saying a single intelligent word, he accomplished his purpose, which was to harass the foundations and to subdue such stirrings of courage, or even of imagination, as could be found in them. As I have said, there were not many there when he came on the scene. Congressman Cox had been there before him. And even before Congressman Cox, the foundations were coming to limit their venturesome risk capital supplying to the natural sciences, medicine, technology, and long-term research. These fields are of great public benefit. They are also not controversial. If there ever was a foundation that was willing to be controversial, that was willing to take risks and to venture capital in areas about which people have strong prejudices, it learned its lesson by the time Cox and Reece got through. Who will venture now?

DANGER ON THE RIGHT *

by Arnold Forster and Benjamin R. Epstein

No ONE really knows how much money is being poured into the American Right Wing every year to support the massive reactionary Rightist propaganda campaign which seeks to influence and to change American political opinion.

Nevertheless, as is pointed out in the opening pages of this book, it is a fair and conservative estimate that the minimum cost of the overall Rightist propaganda assault on the American mind is in the neighborhood of $14,000,000 a year. This encompasses the known expenses of the American Right, ranging from the extremely conservative organization to the Radical Right. It does not include the far-out organizations tainted with racism and anti-Semitism; they raise more than a million dollars for their own special purposes.

A substantial portion of the $14,000,000 that is poured into

* From Danger on the Right (New York: Random House, 1964), pp. 272–277. Danger on the Right was part of a series of books created by the staff of the Anti-Defamation League of B'nai B'rith. Arnold Forster has been the League's General Counsel since 1946. Benjamin Epstein has been with the League since 1939, and in 1956 became its National Commissioner.

extremely conservative and Radical Right propaganda comes this way: from some 70 or more foundations (almost all tax-exempt), 113 business firms and corporations, 25 public utilities, and some 250 individuals who can be identified as having contributed at least $500 each in recent years.

It is unwise, with the imprecise information that can be collected to venture a breakdown of the money supplied to the American Right Wing by each of the three groupings—the foundations, corporations, or the individuals—or by any particular foundation, corporation, or individual. It should also be borne in mind that a considerable proportion of the money comes from small contributors—most of whom do not contribute anything near $500 each.

Included among the seventy-odd foundations are some of the most public-spirited agencies in the United States—agencies whose money nourishes civic, educational, religious, health, and charitable work of the most worthy kind. Their annual outlays for such worth-while causes are, in many cases, of staggering proportions, often millions of dollars. The contributions such giant foundations make to Right Wing causes may perhaps be only a drop in the bucket to them, but surely are of considerable importance to the annual budget of the ordinary Rightist organization. Contributions, for instance, of $1,000, $5,000 or even $25,000 may be a negligible part of a giant foundation's annual giving; they are substantial items to a Rightist group.

Clearly then, with rare exceptions, most of the foundations which contribute to the Right Wing organizations were not set up for the express purpose of financing such causes. Worse still, these gifts to Rightist groups are usually included with grants to schools, to colleges, to churches, and to other recipients whose work is entirely free of any political connotation.

On the other hand, some of the foundations are the creations of individuals or families whose names are to be found among the leaders and sponsors of Rightist organizations. Still other foundations are the creatures of companies whose principals personally support Rightist causes and who often influence their companies to support such Right Wing groups.

Examples are not hard to find. The Chance Foundation in Centralia, Missouri, is the creation of F. Gano Chance, a member of the Birch council and board chairman of the Chance Company. The Grede Foundation, Inc., in Milwaukee, Wisconsin, is the creation of William J. Grede, also a member of the Birch Society national council. The Ada Hearne Foundation in Seviervill, Tennessee, is the outlet for contributions by A. G. Heinsohn, Jr., still another Birch council member, and a principal in Spindale and Cherokee Mills. And the Harnischfeger Foundation of Milwaukee is the creation of the Harnischfeger Corporation and of Walter Harnischfeger, who has for a number of years given support to Right Wing organizations.

These very foundations support worth-while civic work, but their contributions also go to Right Wing organizations. The Chance Foundation, for example, in recent years, sent generous gifts to the Hargis Christian Crusade, the Schwarz Christian Anti-Communism Crusade, McIntire's American Council of Christian Churches, as well as to the Intercollegiate Society of Individualists, Harding College, and America's Future, Inc.

Some foundations appear sometimes to allocate a *major* portion of their annual giving to Rightist causes. During 1959, for instance, Heinsohn's very modest Ada Hearne Foundation made total contributions of a little over $20,000. Almost $15,000 of that total went to the American Economic Foundation and the Christian Freedom Foundation, $1,000 each went to Harding College, the Intercollegiate Society of Individualists, and to the National Foundation for Education in American Citizenship—the latter a major source of funds in recent years for *Human Events*. Against this, some $200 went to the Knoxville Symphony Society, $100 to Smith College, $500 to a Baptist school, and another $1,500 went to two churches.

The O'Donnell Foundation of Dallas, heavily financed by Peter O'Donnell, Jr., a leading supporter of Senator Goldwater for President, has also channeled a fair proposition of its annual outlays to Rightists' purposes. In fiscal 1962, for instance, when O'Donnell Foundation grants totaled $65,000, $20,000 went to the Intercollegiate Society of Individualists, which had received a total of $10,000 in two earlier years.

Sometimes, the stated purposes for which a foundation is created make its objective quite clear. For instance, when J. Howard Pew created the J. Howard Pew Freedom Trust in 1957, the statement of purposes in the trust agreement declared:

"Socialism, Welfare-state-ism, Marxism, Fascism and any other like forms of government intervention are but devices by which government seizes the ownership or control of the tools of production."

It added that the trust would seek to "acquaint the American people with the evils of bureaucracy and the vital need to maintain and preserve a limited form of government." It also would point out the "dangerous consequences that result from an exchange of our priceless American heritage of freedom and self-determination, for the false promises of Socialism and a planned economy" and "expose the insidious influences which have infiltrated many of our channels of publicity." Finally, the foundation planned to acquaint the American people with the values of a free market, the dangers of inflation, and the need for a stable monetary standard.

When the Trust applied for tax exemption in 1958, a year after it was formed, it declared that it sought to make grants to "religious, charitable, and scientific, literary or educational organizations . . . to be used for the teaching on the meaning of individual liberty and freedom." During the calendar year 1962, $24,000 of the $59,000 spent by the J. Howard Pew Freedom Trust went to the Christian Freedom Foundation ($20,000), the Foundation for Economic Education ($2,000) and the American Economic Foundation ($2,000). . . .

With the caveat that any example of foundation support for the American Right Wing is not necessarily typical of its giving, and that any foundation named may also support the most worthwhile causes, it is possible to cite some revealing examples of foundation support for Rightist causes, some of which have been mentioned elsewhere in this book:

ITEM: The large contributions by the Alfred P. Sloan Foundation of New York to Dr. Benson's establishment on the campus of Harding College in Searcy, Arkansas, helped launch Benson's National Education Program of today. Other foundation money has helped keep it going—for instance, $38,000 from the Donner Foundation of Philadelphia in 1959 and 1960.

ITEM: In the fiscal year 1961–62, the William Volker Fund of Burlingame, California (now being liquidated), donated $48,066.50 to the Intercollegiate Society of Individualists. The Lilly Endowment supplied $25,000, the Marquette Charitable Organization $19,000, the Relm Foundation $5,-000, Curran Foundation $3,000, the Ingersoll Foundation $4,050, and the Ada Hearne and Deering Milliken Foundations $2,500 each. There were numerous other, and smaller, foundation grants to ISI. Of a total income from contributions of $181,616.00 for the fiscal year, the Intercollegiate Society of Individualists received $129,404.85 in foundation funds.

ITEM: In the five-year period, 1956 to 1961, the William Volker Fund contributed almost $270,000 to the Council for Basic Education, Washington, D.C. The Council has received frequent favorable mention in the Right Wing publication *Human Events*, which has reprinted articles from the Council Bulletin attacking "progressive" education and the "unethical practice" of teachers joining "professional" organizations. The Council also opposes Federal aid to education. (In 1958, the first phase of a "basic curriculum study" by the Council was financed by a $34,000 grant from the Relm Foundation, Ann Arbor, Michigan.) In the same five-year period, 1956 to 1961, the Volker Fund also contributed more than $320,000 to the Foundation for Voluntary Welfare, of which $192,887 was contributed in fiscal 1960, when Medicare was a major issue on the national scene. The Volker Fund also has served as a source of support for research and writing in the social sciences by economists and scholars of Rightist viewpoint, like Ludwig von Mises, and it heavily underwrote the distribution of "basic books" to college libraries over a period of years.

ITEM: During 1958–62, $125,000 was contributed to Dr. Fred Schwarz's Christian Anti-Communism Crusade via the Glenmede Trust Company of Philadelphia, which serves as trustee for Pew Foundation funds.

ITEM: More than $30,000 of Pew Foundation money was contributed between 1958 and 1962 to the Christian Freedom Foundation. (The overwhelming bulk of the Christian Freedom Foundation's annual budget is supplied by individual contributions from Mr. J. Howard Pew and Mrs. Mabel Pew Myrin, whose donations to the CFF between 1958 and 1962 were well over $1,000,000.) The CFF is not, itself, a foundation in the sense that it provides grants and other contributions. It is, rather, a recipient of funds which it expends on its own activities.

ITEM: Between 1955 and 1961, the Donner Foundation, Philadelphia, Pennsylvania, contributed $95,000 to the American Economic Foundation. Between 1958 and 1961, the Donner Foundation gave $57,500 to the American Enterprise Association, now called the American Enterprise Institute for Public Policy Research. In 1956 and 1957, the Donner group contributed a total of $50,000 to Americans for the Competitive Enterprise System.

ITEM: The Relm Foundation of Ann Arbor, Michigan, whose resources are somewhat smaller than those of many other foundations, has nevertheless consistently supported a number of Right Wing groups. Between 1957 and 1960, the Relm Foundation gave $38,800 to the American Economic Foundation, $8,500 to the American Enterprise Association, almost $25,000 to the Council for Basic Education, $29,500 to the Foundation for Economic Education.

ITEM: As noted in this book, the National Foundation for Education in American Citizenship, Inc., Indianapolis, Indiana, has for some years been a consistent supporter of the Right Wing newsletter, *Human Events*, and these contributions appear to be the largest single item of annual expenditure by the Foundation. For the years 1957 to 1962 inclusive, the National Foundation for Education in American Citizenship gave a reported $330,000 to *Human Events*. In recent years, more than 90 percent of contributions made by the Foundation went to *Human Events*.

The foregoing few instances of how foundation funds are channeled into organizations and propaganda arms of the American Right Wing are obviously only examples.

CHARITY BEGINS AT HOME: FOUNDATIONS AS A TAX DODGE *

by Fred J. Cook

NEITHER PATMAN nor anyone else denies that the original foundation idea was a lofty one or that many foundations, when they adhered to the charitable purposes for which they were created, have been expressive of the finest traditions of American idealism. They have financed advances in education, in medicine, in science; they have done inestimable good. But in many cases they have used their special tax-exempt privileges and their hoarded millions for ends that bear not the faintest resemblance to charity.

Let's take an outstanding example of the manner in which the American public, which must pay heavier taxes to make up for those the foundations do not pay, finances its own brainwashing at the hands of foundations dedicated to spreading the fantasies of the ultra-Right.

In 1940 there was incorporated in Indiana an organization known as the National Foundation for Education in American Citizenship (NFEAC). Its purposes sounded appropriately lofty—"To make better known the American way of

* "Charity Begins at Home: Foundations as a Tax Dodge," *The Nation*, 196(April 20, 1963), 321–323. Fred J. Cook is a prolific writer in the muckraking tradition. A former award-winning newspaperman, he is a frequent contributor to *The Nation* magazine.

life among adults, college, high school and elementary school children by grants to writers of books, pamphlets, and addresses dealing with the American theme; by fostering observation of patriotic holidays; by bringing outstanding speakers on education and political subjects."

Much of the original financing was supplied by J. K. Lilly, a scion of the drug firm of Eli Lilly & Co., long a supporter of right-wing causes, as the Buchanan committee's investigation of corporate lobbying showed in 1950. At that time, it was disclosed that Eli Lilly & Co. had contributed $25,000 to the hard-Right Committee for Constitutional Government, which has disseminated literature frowning on the forty-hour week, collective bargaining and Social Security and other welfare legislation.

Contributions that a corporation makes to such propaganda and lobbying fronts may be questionable enough, but the questions are compounded when the foundation device is used as a tax-escape hatch for the same propagandistic endeavors. What happened to the money funneled into the NFEAC by Lilly and other arch-conservative interests? The records are incomplete, but such as they are, they show that more than 88 per cent of it went to finance *Human Events*, a weekly ultra-Right sheet that because of its propagandistic nature, could not possibly qualify for tax exemption.

There is nothing to indicate what the NFEAC did with its funds in the first ten years of its existence. Internal Revenue records for those years have been destroyed, and so the available reports begin with 1951. Even these are incomplete: there is a four-year blank from 1954 through 1957. . . . The gap means that Internal Revenue can account for NFEAC's financial activities in only seven of the last eleven years. This accounting shows that, for those years, the foundation had at its disposal funds totaling $414,835; that it spent $379,790; and that, of this amount, $232,310—more than 88 per cent of all non-administrative expenditures—went to *Human Events.* From 1958 through 1961, the figure was 95 to 98 per cent. Typical was 1958, when the foundation contributed $5 to the New York Department of Social Welfare—and $47,360 to *Human Events.*

Stark as such figures are, they tell only part of the story. Returns filed by the foundation with the Secretary of State of Indiana do not agree in all respects with those filed with Internal Revenue. The most glaring discrepancy occurred in 1961, when the foundation reported to Internal Revenue that it had contributed $45,038 to *Human Events*—and to the State of Indiana that it had contributed $72,408. In all, the Indiana returns for 1957 and 1962 increase the figures available from Internal Revenue to show that, in the last six years, the foundation bankrolled *Human Events* to the extent of $329,661.

The prolonged love affair between the NFEAC and *Human Events* is a liaison, however, that exposes more than itself. It opens a window on a whole nest of ultra-Right activities that are financed to a great extent with tax-exempt, foundation funds. For instance, Felix Morley, one of the early directors of NFEAC and a former president of *Human Events,* has since become secretary of Admiral Ben Moreell's Americans for Constitutional Action, whose *Voting Record Index* interpreting the actions of Congressmen is the bible of the radical Right. The index, which achieved its greatest notoriety when it was disclosed that Birchite Maj. Gen. Edwin A. Walker was using it to indoctrinate his troops in Germany, is compiled and distributed by *Human Events.*

Human Events has also had a close relationship with the Life Line Foundation, the creation of Texas oil billionaire H.

L. Hunt. Until recently, the two organizations shared the same Washington headquarters. Life Line Foundation was established in 1958 by the simple process of amending the corporate charter of Facts Forum, Hunt's original right-wing propaganda package, into which he had poured some $219,000 (tax exempt). Life Line Foundation, featuring the daily radio program of suave preacher-commentator, the Rev. Wayne Poucher, combines religion and patriotism with right-wing doctrine in a heady mixture that is carried by more than 200 radio stations in twenty-eight states.

Such weddings of foundation-interests are to be found throughout the entire NFEAC–*Human Events* relationship. Even incomplete records (NFEAC, despite laws to the contrary, never listed its contributors) show how foundations contributed to foundations so that the money, passing from one tax-exempt institution to another, finally wound up in the coffers of non-tax-exempt *Human Events*. The linkage tells its own significant story.

Take, for example, the Texas Educational Association, headed by George Van Horn Moseley, who has been characterized as a nationalistic propagandist, and George W. Armstrong, Jr., an editorial adviser to the Birch Society magazine and an endorser of the Manion Forum. This Texas organization sent $900 a year in 1960 and 1961 to NFEAC mailing its contribution directly to 408 First Street, S.E., Washington, D.C., the address of *Human Events*—a deed, it would seem, that recognized that the foundation and its shadow were one. Other foundations similarly channeled money into *Human Events* through the intermediary of tax-exempt NFEAC. In 1956, 1957 and 1958, the Deering Milliken Foundation, of New York, supported by certain textile interests, funneled $1,500 a year into NFEAC.

In 1952, the William Volker Fund, of Burlingame, Calif., contributed $5,000 to NFEAC, a donation apparently earmarked specifically for *Human Events*. The Volker Fund, incorporated in Missouri in 1932 with the proceeds of a home-furnishing business, has been a large and influential promoter of right-wing causes. In 1957 alone, it made grants of $823,-099, including one of $3,000 to Felix Morley. Other recipients in that year were the American Enterprise Association, which received $5,000, and the Foundation for Economic Education, which got $10,000.

The Foundation for Economic Education, another far-Right tub-thumper that is supported by tax-free funds largely contributed by big corporations, publishes *The Freeman*, which touts itself as a "nonpolitical, nonprofit educational champion of private property." Both *The Freeman* and its parent foundation had been favorites of NFEAC. In fact, the second largest "charity" contribution NFEAC ever made, outside of its annual bequests to *Human Events*, was a 1953 donation of $7,935 to *The Freeman*.

Such cross-ties and proliferating bequests that water right-wing propaganda causes are obviously a far cry from the law's definition of a tax-exempt charity as any group "organized and operated *exclusively* for religious, charitable, scientific, literary or educational purposes or for the prevention of cruelty to children or animals."

It is ironical that, to date, virtually the only outcry that has ever been raised against the foundations for perverting "charity" into propaganda came after the Ford Foundation, in 1953, set up The Fund for the Republic with a $15 million fund to do battle for our "constitutional liberties," which were then being shot full of holes by the McCarthyites. The conservative press howled with alarm, and there was much gnashing of teeth and many dire threats about imposing curbs on foundations because they were becoming a Red menace to the Republic. Even today The Fund for the Republic is frequently flaunted as an example of the "left-wing" foundation menace, but the silence of the grave shrouds the much more prolific abuse by the powerful complex of right-wing foundations. Behind this screen of secrecy and silence, however, doubtless lies the reason why, despite all the agitation about The Fund for the Republic, no real action has ever been initiated to curb foundation propagandizing. The radical Right has too vital a stake in the brainwashing process.

The power and influence that protect such right-wing propagandizing are perhaps best illustrated by the caution with which Internal Revenue has acted. Although Internal Revenue (on the basis of such reports as were available to it) had been put on notice as early as 1951 that 40 per cent of the contributions of the National Foundation for Education in American Citizenship were then going into *Human Events*, no action was taken for more than a decade. Not until late 1962, when some Congressmen began to question the propriety of continuing this tax-exempt charity, did Internal Revenue move. Then, on October 10, 1962, it announced quietly that it was revoking NFEAC's tax-exempt status; but it refused to make public the results of its findings or its plans—if any—for invoking penalties.

A comparably gingerly approach has marked Internal Revenue's dealings with the tax-exempt National Education Program set up by Dr. George S. Benson at Harding College in Searcy, Ark. The program, which was granted tax-exempt status in 1954, has been widely recognized as the brain trust of the ultra-Right. The controversial and distorted film *Communism on the Map* was one of its more notable products. Details about N.E.P.'s finances have remained somewhat obscure, however, because, according to Internal Revenue, none of the required forms had been filed from 1954 to 1961. But Internal Revenue acknowledged frankly that nobody had ever been punished for failure to live up to requirements of the Foundation Act, which provides for strict accounting of contributions and the use to which they are put.

FOUNDATION PIPE LINES:
THE BENEFICENT CIA *

by Robert G. Sherrill

ONE OF the "in" games in Washington is uncovering the funny business of the Central Intelligence Agency, especially as it relates to funneling money through a maze of foundations for the purpose of shaping foreign policy. Last month Group Research, Inc., a fact-finding organization based in Washington, made a high score in this game by picking up a cold trail (a couple of years old, thanks to the Internal Revenue Service's tardiness in assimilating and releasing such data). It was nevertheless a significant trail, because it appeared to lead to the American Friends of the Middle East, an anti-Zionist, pro-Arab, organization; and to the Cuban Freedom Committee, sponsor of "Free Cuba Radio" and certainly the most belligerent anti-Castro radio series broadcast out of this country, whose advisory board includes several galloping right wingers.

* "Foundation Pipe Lines: The Beneficent CIA," *The Nation*, 202 (May 9, 1966), 542–544, 556. Robert G. Sherrill is on the staff of *The Nation*.

Followers of this mystery serial may recall that two years ago Rep. Wright Patman of Texas, investigating the CIA–Kaplan Fund–IRS arrangement, demanded information relating to eight other foundations. [See editorial, "Foundations as 'Fronts,' " *The Nation*, September 14, 1964.] The Kaplan Fund, he had discovered by stubborn detective work, was a conduit for CIA funds, and these other eight foundations had been contributing to the Kaplan Fund; so Patman wanted to know if they were part of the CIA pipe line.

At that point he ran into what he called "a hint that I had better not touch this because it involves foreign operations of the CIA." Taking the hint, he rang down the curtain and the rest of his inquiry was finished in executive session. The public learned nothing about the eight foundations; the Michigan Fund, the Gotham Foundation, the Price Fund, the Edsel Fund, the Andrew Hamilton Fund, the Bordon Trust, the Beacon Fund and the Kentifield Fund. Now, as a result of Group Research, Inc.'s investigations, one corner of the bureaucratic curtain has been lifted to reveal as neat a performance of fund swapping as one will find in the IRS files.

Seven of these foundations (the Michigan Fund does not seem to be involved in this ploy) have been giving money to Christianform and/or the American Friends of the Middle East. The benefactions to the American Friends were transmitted through the Brown Foundation, the Jones-O'Donnell Fund and the Marshall Foundation, and these three, plus six of the seven original donors, also gave to Christianform; the Andrew Hamilton Fund gave directly to Christianform but to none of the three intermediary foundations, and Gotham gave nothing directly to Christianform. If these transactions sound complicated, it must be remembered that fiscal simplicity was probably not the first consideration. The point to be noted is that seven of the eight foundations that are known to have been pumping money into the Kaplan Fund have now been found aiding Christianform and the American Friends. How, then, do the recipients use the money?

Christianform is an organization that dates back to 1949. Its founder and president is Nicholas T. Nonnenmacher (Major, Air Force, ret.), former assistant editor of the right-wing publication *Human Events*. For four years he was staff specialist of the American Legion, assigned to its subversive activities committee, and is now administrative assistant to Glen Andrews of Alabama, one of the more unreconstructed Congressmen. Nonnenmacher's latest achievement was writing the script for the movie, *Peace or Communism*, which gives the peaceniks the usual rough treatment. One notable adviser to Christianform has been Paul Crouch, the professional ex-Communist who left his smudge on several Congressional investigations.

The income of their organization having mysteriously soared from $3,100 in 1959 to more than $250,000 in 1961, the patriots of Christianform spawned the Cuban Freedom Committee and went into the nonprofit business of propagandizing the Cubans and other Latin Americans via three radio stations—WGBS in Miami, WKWF in Key West and WWL in New Orleans. More than 200 hours of propaganda are broadcast from these stations each month, and canned portions of the program are rebroadcast over twenty stations in Latin America.

As with any heated propagandizing effort, Free Cuba Radio often gets tangled in its own tales. Its promotional brochure notes that "today in Cuba in moats, centuries-old fortresses, jails and concentration camps . . . under indescribably unsanitary and filthy conditions, exist more than 50,000 political prisoners, subjected to torture. . . ." Yet in a press release from the organization, one learns that a Cuban "newly arrived in the United States, who was jailed for forty-three days in Havana, related how he and his fellow prisoners listened to the Cuban Freedom Committee programs right under the noses of the guards." (Prisoners were allowed standard radios to listen to Castro and the Communist propaganda.) With what other luxuries are those torture chambers equipped?

However, *aficionados* of Free Cuba Radio are less likely to go to it for precise history than they are for the kind of humor heard on the program, "If It Weren't So Tragic, It Would Be Comic!" A typical quip on a recent program:

Announcer: After he heard of the police raids Fidel had initiated against drinking and other vices, Raul, his brother went to a doctor and begged: "Please, doctor, go tell Fidel that what I have isn't a vice."

Officials of Free Cuba Radio believe that Raul is a homosexual, and this joke is supposed to be an allusion to that. On other occasions the comic announcer will talk about "Mother Raul" and his long hair.

Mrs. Mariada C. Arensberg, executive secretary of the Cuban Freedom Committee and director of the radio propagandists headquartered in Washington, said that this kind of joke is a real knee slapper in Cuba.

Another program tells the Cubans how to sabotage the sugar cane: "Plant the sugar cane seed upside down." And still another offers Cuban military officers the logic that they needn't obey the Castros because "they are politicians, not military men."

Somebody in the United States likes that kind of material

well enough to shell out $400,000 a year, which is what Mrs. Arensberg says the radio assault costs.

Mrs. Arensberg told *The Nation:* "I would just as soon you didn't write about our advisory board," and as for the financing of the radio barrage, she said that comes "from foundations, but I would just as soon you didn't write about that either."

The advisory board displays quite a potpourri of ideologies. It includes Mrs. Oveta Culp Hobby, publisher of the Houston *Post* and once in Eisenhower's Cabinet; Edward G. Miller, former Assistant Secretary of State for Latin American Affairs; Sen. Claiborne Pell of Rhode Island; Rep. Roman C. Pucinski of Illinois; and Walter Williams, former Under Secretary of Commerce.

But the most vocal members of the board are Donald C. Bruce, former Congressman from Indiana (Nonnenmacher was his administrative assistant when he was in Congress); Peter O'Donnell, Dallas businessman; George S. Schuyler, associate editor of the Pittsburgh *Courier*, and John B. McClatchy, Philadelphia businessman and chairman of the advisory committee. Together, they make a shining constellation of ultraconservatives:

¶ Throughout his Congressional career Bruce advocated total naval blockade of Cuba; public support of a "Cuban army of liberation," and recognition of a government-in-exile. He has spoken for the Manion Forum, for Human Events Political Action Conferences, for the Christian Anti-Communism Crusade, and for the National Right-To-Work Committee. He believed President Kennedy "opposed Castro, but not communism."

¶ Board Chairman McClatchy participates in the Human

Events Political Action Conferences and is a life member of Christian Anti-Communism Crusade. He contributed $10,370 to Christianform in 1960, the year Free Cuba Radio was formed—the only individual to make a big money contribution.

¶ For a time, Gen. Albert Wedemeyer, a former member of the advisory board of H. L. Hunt's Life Line and a spokesman at just about every important right-wing gathering, was on the Free Cuba Radio board, but he got sick and quit. The remaining members of the board remember him as "being hard to get along with."

¶ Peter O'Donnell is best known for having led the National Draft Goldwater Committee, but he is also a guiding light for the Young Americans for Freedom and other earnest organizations of the type.

¶ The most interesting member of the board is George S. Schuyler, Negro journalist, who has made something of a name for himself by addressing John Birch conventions on the general theme: Why the South Is a Beautiful Place for Negroes to Live. At a John Birch convention in Denver, in March, he said that when Negroes live in ghettos, they do so because of "the natural human preference." Schuyler was identified with the old China lobby, and he presently is on the advisory committee for the Committee on Pan American Policy, one-fifth of whose members are either on the John Birch Society's national council or on the advisory committee of Rev. Billy James Hargis' Christian Crusade.

In 1962, just prior to the Punta del Este consultation of foreign ministers, called by the Council of the Organization of American States, Mrs. Arensberg wrote letters to Congressmen and Senators in which she urged a tough go-it-alone line: "The fetish of continental unity is hampering the United

States of America in her effort to isolate and to thwart Communist Cuba. . . . The United States of America must go to Punta del Este with a strong policy to defend the inter-American system and to protect this country if left alone."

Much the same sentiments were expressed by Schuyler in an article he wrote in 1965 for the John Birch magazine *American Opinion:* "Our leaders are mentally shackled against any effective action in dealing with the Communist threat in this hemisphere; our hands are tied by preposterous OAS commitments. . . ."

The same zealous enthusiasm to strike out, and to hell with diplomacy, motivates the staff of Free Cuba Radio today. Dr. Herminio Portell-Vila, who writes many of the radio's propaganda programs, says: "I believe in killing Castro. I believe in blowing up Cuba's refineries. These things I believe in doing."

Mrs. Arensberg says: "We do not think in terms of ten years from now. We think in terms of six months. Anything could happen in that time. Castro could be killed. Anything could happen."

The purpose of Free Cuba Radio is to create an atmosphere in which "anything"—including the death of Castro—is more likely to happen, soon.

For fifteen years the American Friends of the Middle East has been operating on the tightrope philosophy that it isn't anti-Israel, it is merely anti-Zionist—a distinction some Jews have had a hard time following. As one of its regional representatives once explained, "Since AFME is frankly pro-Arab, it is necessarily anti-Zionist, but that is its *one and only negative* aspect."

AFME has always been able to point to some "name" officers. The late Dorothy Thompson was a founder. Rev. Harry Emerson Fosdick and William Ernest Hocking have been regulars. Earl Bunting, a former president of the National Association of Manufacturers, has served as chairman of the board of AFME. Eisenhower's pastor, Rev. L. R. Elson, was a national chairman of AFME. While insisting that he was certainly not "anti-Israel," he said he considered its creation to be "a diplomatic debacle." The Reverend Elson also said that the Zionist movement was as foreign to this country as the German-American Bund activities supporting Hitler before World War II.

AFME has always stressed the need to keep the Arab nations soothed in order to safeguard our oil interests in that area. Prominent Senators and Congressmen from oil states turn out for AFME soirees in Washington. On AFME's board is Kermit Roosevelt of Gulf Oil Company and, in his day, quite a government cloak-and-dagger man himself.

Hidden behind an Internal Revenue Service exemption that permits the AFME to keep secret the sources of its income, the anti-Zionist organization has spent money like a drunken sheik. For some time the CIA has been suspected of sinking money in the AFME. The suspicions were around long before Bushrod Howard, Jr., an agent for the Yemeni royalists, told the Senate Foreign Relations Committee in 1963: "Some are putting all the blame for the problem of the Middle East on Israel and American Jews. To counter these alleged evils they have, over the years, put some $4 million of government funds into an anti-Israel organization."

For some reason the committee didn't ask—and he didn't volunteer to say publicly—who "they" are or what the anti-Israel organization is. But many who follow the undercurrents of Middle Eastern affairs felt the answer to both was pretty obvious. The State Department, of course, issued a memorandum saying: "There is no factual basis for Mr. Howard's charge that U.S. officials support an anti-Israel organization."

The amounts going into the American Friends of the Middle East as uncovered by Group Research, Inc., are minuscule when compared to the $4 million rumor (they come to only $100,000); but at least they help fill out the history of the fund-channeling and put the State Department's demurrer in a questionable light. Up to now only the Dearborn Foundation and the San Jacinto Foundation, the latter a legitimate one (meaning, not a dummy for the CIA) backed by a Texas oil man, had been trailed into the tent of the AFME. These previous discoveries were made by I. L. Kenen, editor of *The Near East Report*.

Now, despite the hedging of those sly dogs in the IRS and the CIA, we know three more foundations that pump money into the anti-Zionist work. They are the Brown Foundation, the Jones-O'Donnell Foundation, and the Marshall Foundation. We also know that *those* foundations, in turn, received large donations from five other foundations which were cornered by Patman in the CIA-Kaplan gambit. There must be many other conduit foundations involved, so the game has really only begun.

U.S. PHILANTHROPIC FOUNDATIONS: THEIR HISTORY, STRUCTURE, MANAGEMENT, AND RECORD *

by Warren Weaver

MUCH OF the value to our society of philanthropic foundations comes from their independent status. They are not "government controlled" as regards their choice of projects and their freedom to say what they please. It is difficult to enter into any sort of collaboration with government, however amiably conceived, without unexpected and creeping involvement. A high officer of a major foundation was asked by the State Department to act as the chairman of a group to survey certain needs and opportunities in a foreign, underdeveloped area. The group of technical experts chosen by the foundation official were accompanied on the trip by State Department officers. Before departure, the foundation officer was

* From *U.S. Philanthropic Foundations: Their History, Structure, Management, and Record* (New York: Harper & Row, 1967; copyright © 1967 by the American Academy of Arts and Sciences), pp. 191–194. Warren Weaver taught mathematics at the California Institute of Technology and the University of Wisconsin before becoming a director and vice president of the Rockefeller Foundation. In his own words, "In addition to twenty-eight years of experience as an officer of the Rockefeller Foundation followed by seven years as vice president and as a special consultant of the Alfred P. Sloan Foundation, I have had, concurrently, more than twenty-five years' experience in eight other foundations and federal granting agencies such as the National Science Foundation and the National Institutes of Health."

quietly informed that he must take his tuxedo. Now this sounds silly, but the point is that it *was* silly. At every stop, valuable time was taken up with formalities essentially useless from the point of view of the technical experts.

Much more serious, and more subtle, involvements can occur. During the period in the early forties when the Russians were our allies, two very distinguished Russian scientists, with the enthusiastic approval of our government, visited the United States as the guests of the Rockefeller Foundation. At a farewell party, the conversation took a friendly and confidential turn. They indicated a wish to ask some questions which had been troubling them, and they were encouraged to do so. What was their first question? It was "What is the interrelation of the Rockefeller Foundation with your government?" When told that apart from a minimum of formal requirements for reporting, there simply *was* no relationship— no control, no consultation—the Russians found this hard to believe.

A prominent physicist, writing to the Sloan Foundation in praise of its fellowship program, said, "Last June when we had some prominent Soviet scientist-administrators here for a disarmament discussion, I tried to explain the Ford Foundation's support for that effort to them, with its special mixture of public responsibility and private initiative. As far as I could interpret their reactions, they just don't understand the complementarity between private and government funds, and my guess is that when they finally do we won't need disarmament conferences!"

But that lack of governmental involvement, however long it has sometimes taken for it to be fully credited, has been of inestimable value in working in foreign countries. A foundation officer is accepted as an intellectual comrade, with no complication from political formalities. The collaboration can be far stickier than the two above examples would indicate. During World War II a suggestion was made that, in certain "sensitive" geographical areas, the public health personnel of the Rockefeller Foundation could, so to speak, "keep their eyes open" and then report to our government. These medical men were highly qualified as to language and knowledge of local customs, and they were absolutely trusted by the foreign populations. But they were so trusted precisely because the trust had never been abused. However discreetly phrased, the request sought in fact to have these men act in a spying capacity.

The request for this kind of "collaboration with government" was resolutely and firmly refused. Even when the request was repeated, with more authority behind it, it was refused. And it should have been.

The issues—and the potential difficulties—raised by collaboration between foundations and government have been dramatically illustrated by the recent disclosures that the Central Intelligence Agency has used certain foundations . . . as conduits for government money that ended up supporting a wide variety of overseas educational and cultural activities.

There were four steps to this process. First, the CIA received from the government funds over which the agency had a remarkable, if not indeed a unique, degree of unsupervised control.

Second, these funds were transferred to various foundations. The list may well not be complete, but there appear to be at least thirty-eight foundations involved in this way. Of these, twenty were concerned with only one activity, eight were involved twice, four were involved three times (The

Baird, Borden, Norman, and Benjamin Rosenthal foundations), four were involved four times (The Gotham, Hobby, Price, and Rabb foundations), and two were involved six times (The J. Frederick Brown Foundation and the Pappas Charitable Trust). It seems that no one of the large and well-known foundations was involved.

These foundations, moreover, merely passed the funds along to a third set of agencies (some fifteen of them), which in turn disbursed the funds to the final recipient organizations or activities, which were very numerous. It is hard to avoid the conclusion that this complication and indirection were deliberately intended to reduce visibility.

The agencies receiving the funds from the foundations included the National Education Association, The National Student Association, The American Newspaper Guild, The American Federation of State, County and Municipal Employees, The Institute for International Labor Research, American Friends of the Middle East, and at least nine others. The final disbursers of the funds included the Association of Hungarian Students in North America, The International Commission of Jurists in Geneva, the Institute of Political Education in Costa Rica, The Center of Studies and Documentation in Mexico, and Radio Free Europe. The final activities thus supported were geographically spread over Latin America, Germany, Africa, and the Middle East. Lawyers, educators, universities, journalists, artists, writers, and students were final recipients. By the time the money emerged to the surface, the original source was pretty thoroughly concealed.

The Hobby Foundation appears to have played a double role, in that they received funds directly from the CIA which they turned over to other agencies, and that they also received funds from some five other foundations (who in turn had received the money from the CIA) and then disbursed these funds to operating agencies.

The complete and dependable details of this fantastic mishmash have not come to the surface as yet, and very probably never will. But enough has emerged to warrant several comments.

First, it appears that the vast majority of the activities ultimately aided, and perhaps all of them, were decent, constructive, and desirable. Second, it seems clear that most, if indeed not all, of the foundations, groups, and agencies were innocent of any improper intent, and in many instances were doubtless unaware of the complicated web of which they were a part. Third, this is a ridiculous and potentially a thoroughly bad way in which to finance good activities. Fourth, the role of the CIA in this matter seems deplorable indeed. If, as has been claimed, the ultimate aid went only to individuals, groups, or agencies that were approved by the CIA, then the foundations that played an intermediate role are to be severely criticized for accepting funds subject to that type of external control.

All in all, this is an example of a very bad kind of collaboration between philanthropic foundations and government.

THE ROONEY REFORM *

by Kenneth Crawford

FOR UNTOLD years there has been talk in Washington about tax reform—closing the loopholes through which the rich and

* "The Rooney Reform," *Newsweek*, 73 (March 3, 1969), 29. Kenneth Crawford is a columnist for *Newsweek* magazine.

the wily escape payment of their fair share of the cost of government. It is easier to talk than to do. But now, at last, the House Ways and Means Committee has started the painful process of doing. Hearings it is conducting will take weeks and debate in the House and Senate will go on for months.

Which among the many proposed reforms will survive the protracted legislative ordeal can only be guessed at this early in the proceedings. However, one guess can be ventured with some assurance after only a few days of advocacy by witnesses appearing before chairman Wilbur Mills and his Ways and Means colleagues. It is that tax-exempt foundations will be forbidden to dabble in politics, directly or indirectly, on pain of losing their tax-exempt status.

This prohibition was all but guaranteed by Rep. John J. Rooney of Brooklyn, who, although not himself a member of the Mills committee, made a distinct impression upon it. He did this by recounting his experience in the 1968 election. What happened, he said, was that a rich interloper from a silk-stocking district in Manhattan had the gall and the gelt to make a bid for the Congressional seat Rooney has occupied for the last quarter century. Worse than the gall was the gelt, he declared, at least the part of it that came from a privileged foundation.

Rooney's is not a household name in the United States or even in Washington, but it is in State Department and in diplomatic households. As chairman of the subcommittee in charge of State Department and overseas U.S. Embassy expenditures, he is their scourge, if not their Scrooge. No American ambassador spends a tax dollar which, in Rooney's opinion, could be saved. Sometimes his economies are arbitrary, even outrageous, but he makes them stick.

In the opinion of some, Rooney is symbolic of what's

wrong with Congress. But in Congress itself his seniority and political skills, refined by 25 years of politicking in the Capitol and in his waterfront district, command a certain respect. He looks like an inoffensive leprechaun, but his associates never make the mistake of judging him by his appearance. He is effective on his own ground, never more so than he was in his appearance before Ways and Means.

"I am the first known member of Congress to be forced to campaign for re-election against the awesome financial resources of a tax-exempt foundation," he said. "This time it happened in my district. It can—and probably will—happen in your districts. In the appeal of this political gimmick is a threat to every officeholder, in Congress or elsewhere, who does not have access to a fat bankroll or to a business or to a tax-exempt foundation."

Naturally, Rooney's point was well taken by congressmen who will be up for re-election in 1970. They paid attention as he told how Frederick W. Richmond, whom he described as an affluent New Yorker with a yen for Brooklyn politics, established a charitable foundation several years ago. Rooney didn't object to this but he did object when the Frederick W. Richmond Foundation started concentrating on ethnic-minority causes in his district and advertising its benefactions. The recipients included a Talmudic academy, a Puerto Rican child-care center, several Catholic organizations, a Spanish society and, finally, Neighborhood Study Clubs.

"In actuality, this organization [Neighborhood Study Clubs, Inc.] was nothing more than Richmond's version of the old neighborhood ward clubs," Rooney said. "Almost $43,000 was pumped into Neighborhood Study Clubs by the Frederick W. Richmond Foundation and various friends of Richmond."

Rooney read the committee a New York Times article quoting Richmond to the effect that he was running "the first well-financed campaign in the history of Brooklyn" and not disputing reports that "he has spent $250,000 in this [1968] campaign."

"How did Richmond manage to scrape up this kind of money for a campaign kitty?" Rooney asked. "Right out of the taxpayers' pockets [through tax exemption], that's how he did it."

The tax reform bill almost certainly will impose tighter restrictions on tax-exempt foundations, especially against political activity. Even the mighty Ford Foundation finds itself under fire for granting $131,000 to former employees of Robert Kennedy.

FOUNDATIONS UNDER ATTACK *

by Whitney M. Young, Jr.

AT THIS time, when we hear so much about how important it is for the private sector to become involved in voluntary efforts, a major attack has been launched on organizations doing just that.

Proposed changes in the tax laws include provisions that could just about wipe out any meaningful work for social progress by foundations.

The proposals include: a five percent tax on foundation income, a ban on voter education programs, and a ban on at-

* A syndicated column, which appeared in the Colorado Springs Free Press, July 20, 1969. Whitney M. Young, Jr. has been Executive Director of the tax-exempt National Urban League since 1961.

tempts to influence government decisions. There are others, too, but these are the most damaging.

The proposed tax on income would yield only about $60 million and probably cost more to collect than it would bring in. But schools, hospitals, and other beneficiaries of foundation grants would feel the pinch. And the government would probably have to spend even more money to take up the slack caused by reduced foundation support of such institutions.

The ban on voter education drives is totally unjustified. The creation of an informed electorate and the education of citizens to get them to register and vote is something the government itself should be doing. Instead, it's been left to foundations to support such projects.

A democracy can only survive if its citizens take an active interest in political questions and vote. Stopping the foundations from such activities can only increase voter apathy and nonparticipation. And it might even lead some to believe that social change can't be accomplished by the ballot.

Preventing foundations from "influencing government decisions" is also ridiculous. It's so vague that it can be interpreted to mean that a foundation couldn't sponsor a meeting on a social problem, for fear that a government official may attend and be "influenced."

Internal Revenue regulations already on the books stop foundations from lobbying openly or giving their support to those whose major efforts are overtly political. Simple enforcement of these is enough to stop whatever abuses exist.

Other abuses, such as creation of private foundations as a tax dodge for the wealthy can easily be handled by whatever law or regulation is required. And the foundations themselves have proposed that a new office be set up to regulate such activity.

But if the new law isn't aimed at the minor abuses that may exist by some fringe foundations, why has it been proposed?

It appears to be a politically inspired effort to punish foundations for their newly discovered interest in racial and urban problems.

Several foundations have pioneered in voter registration drives among black people in urban centers and in the South. They've also supported civil rights groups and others interested in making democracy work.

So the word has gone out among the backlashers: Punish the foundations. But the real loser is the country.

The major contribution foundations have made is to support new ideas and programs; the kinds of things others, especially governments, have been unwilling to take a chance on. Without foundations, there might never have been public libraries, teachers pensions, better health facilities, cures for malaria and other diseases, or educational television.

While black people were being fire-hosed and beaten in the South, and while the government was wringing its hands trying to figure out what was to be done, foundations were tooling up to tackle the major problems affecting black people.

If some foundations are abusing their tax-exempt status, regulate them. But don't punish all foundations by short-sighted punitive steps that can only result in great harm to the vitally important role they play in our national life.

Part Four

Business and Taxes

HOUSE REPORT ON TAX-EXEMPT FOUNDATIONS AND CHARITABLE TRUSTS *

OUR STUDY establishes the fact that there is a pressing need for an immediate moratorium on the granting of tax exemptions to foundations, for the following reasons:

1. Laxness and irresponsibility on the part of the Internal Revenue Service.

2. Violations of law and Treasury regulations by far too many of the foundations encompassed in our study.

3. The withdrawal of almost $7 billion from the reach of the tax collectors for taxable years 1951 through 1960. This amount represents the total receipts of only 534 out of an estimated 45,124 tax-exempt foundations.

4. The rapidly increasing concentration of economic power in foundations which—in my view—is far more dan-

* *Tax-Exempt Foundations and Charitable Trusts: Their Impact on our Economy. Chairman's Report to the Select Committee on Small Business,* U.S. House of Representatives 87th Cong. (Washington, D.C.: U.S. Government Printing Office, 1962), pp. 1–5, 8–10, 13, and 15–18. Wright Patman has represented the First District of Texas in Congress since 1929. He has been Chairman of the Banking and Currency Committee, Chairman of the Subcommittee on Domestic Finance, Chairman of the Subcommittee on Small Business, Chairman of the Select Committee on Small Business' Subcommittee on Foundations, Chairman of the Joint Committee On Defense Production, and Vice Chairman of the Joint Economic Committee, among other Congressional assignments.

gerous than anything that has happened in the past in the way of concentration of economic power.

5. Foundation-controlled enterprises possess the money and competitive advantages to eliminate the small businessman.

But first, I should like to detail the background, purposes, and procedures of our study.

The rapid growth in the number and size of tax-exempt foundations has been readily apparent for some years. The Internal Revenue Service reports an increase in numbers from 12,295 at the close of 1952 to a total of 45,124 at the end of 1960—nearly a fourfold increase in 9 years. These figures may be incomplete. We do not know how many hundreds— or thousands—of foundations are in operation without the knowledge of the Treasury, but are nevertheless exempt from Federal income taxation and significant to our study.

This study is an immediate outgrowth of a special survey which I initiated as an individual Member in August 1961 when I directed an inquiry to over 500 foundations requesting certain information. Shortly before the end of the 1st session of the 87th Congress, the Small Business Committee agreed to make the study a committee function, and at the first meeting of the committee in 1962 an authorizing resolution was passed. . . .

Any adequate study of the impact of tax-exempt foundations on our economy and on small business must include a study of their income, the sources of that income, and trends; it must include a record of the expenditures and the purposes for which they are made, including a record of stock manipulations and intercorporate dealings to assure the Congress and the public that the end is "charitable" and not mercenary; it must include a study of the assets of these organizations both as to size and kind, including the holding or acquisition of assets for other than charitable purposes, not excluding the temptation to use foundations for purposes of corporate control, securing special favors, endowing relatives, and contriving to utilize economic power of foundations to create unfair competitive conditions; it must include a study of the extent, if any, to which large corporations are using foundations to evade taxes, however legally, to the detriment of their smaller competitors; and, in the process of securing some or all of the answers to these questions, we have and will inevitably reveal the gaps in laws and regulations or the failure to enforce the laws or regulations which have caused or may cause damage to the economy and small business.

The study revolves around the possible exploitation of the people's respect and admiration for charitable acts and gifts. Are foundations being used as a cloak and a vehicle for crippling competition and accelerating concentration of economic power? Are foundations being used to facilitate the use of economic power, disguised as charity, to attain ends never intended by the people or the Congress—ends such as taking control of commercial enterprises?

The purpose of our study is to determine what the facts are, and to ascertain whether new regulations, or legislation, or better enforcement, are needed to protect small business and to serve the public interest.

The period covered begins with taxable year 1951 and ends with taxable year 1960—for which tax returns were filed in 1952 and 1961 respectively. However, all the foundations do not have a 10-year history, in which case the period covered will be shorter. Some foundations, even though they have a history of 10 years or longer, failed to furnish complete information for the full period.

We have attempted to accurately record all data for the period under study, as furnished to us by the foundations. We have not checked out the arithmetic on the documents submitted by those organizations.

There is no thought of partisanship.

We have secured information from 534 tax-exempt foundations. Our inquiries were sent to a cross section of such organizations. They were not the 534 largest foundations. A number of smaller ones were selected for sampling purposes. Indeed, there is no way of telling which are the 534 largest foundations in the country without examining the annual tax reports of all of them.

We went directly to the foundations because that was the only way to secure information adequate for our purposes. The information available in the files of the Internal Revenue Service was inadequate.

So we directed our inquiries to the recipients of this tax-exemption privilege. We asked the foundations for copies of exemption applications, Internal Revenue Service letters granting exemption, tax returns . . . , accountant's financial statements, investment portfolios, information on directors, trustees, and officers, as well as other financial and legal information for the years 1951 through 1960. After several months, we have most of the material on 534 organizations for this 10-year period, or some portion thereof, if the foundation was created after 1951. . . .

Obtaining the information from the foundations has been a struggle. In many cases, it has taken four or five letters and a reminder of the committee's subpena power to obtain the information needed for this study. Many foundations have taken from 30 to 60 days to reply to a letter. We have been compelled to issue subpenas to 17 of them who failed to furnish information requested. . . .

The attitudes of far too many of the foundations under

study suggest an unmatched arrogance and contempt for the Congress and the people whom we represent. They appear to have adopted the attitude that tax exemption is their birthright —rather than a privilege granted to them by the people, through the Congress, for a public purpose.

The reluctance to cooperate takes many forms. Some only furnished information under subpena, demonstrating something less than a charitable attitude toward public knowledge and democratic processes. Others have sent us incomplete, or partially or wholly illegible, documents. Frequently, principal officers seemed to be in Europe when our letters arrived, leaving no one in the office with access to the records.

Our committee has produced the first penetrating, meaningful insight into the income of a substantial number of tax-exempt foundations—534 out of an estimated 45,124. Many of you will recall that the Reece committee found it impossible to arrive at any accurate estimate of the number of foundations, their income, expenditures, and assets. Foundations give wide publicity to their disbursements—contributions, gifts, grants, etc.—but they seem reluctant to advertise their income.

On the basis of our discoveries thus far, and in view of the rapidly increasing number of tax-exempt foundations, I strongly urge the Secretary of the Treasury to declare an immediate moratorium on granting exemptions to foundations and charitable trusts until such time as the Congress has an opportunity to consider and develop new law and procedures to fit present day economic circumstances and needs.

This recommendation is not made lightly. It is not made casually. It is made in the interest of the taxpaying public and in the interest of good administration and orderly procedures. It is also made in the interest of equal justice.

How can the Treasury Department possibly justify continuing to wring heavy taxes out of the farmer, the worker, and the small businessman, knowing that people of large means are building one foundation after another, and—for all the Treasury knows—for the purpose of decreasing their taxes, eliminating competition and small business, subsidizing antidemocratic propaganda, and otherwise working a hardship on the Nation. This "mess"—and it is a mess—cannot be cleaned up overnight, and many of the people who are now faced with the cleaning job are by no means responsible for this sorry state of affairs but, in the interim, good faith requires that we put an end to the spiraling number of these tax-free entities until we can bring some degree of order into these matters and assure the people that their taxes are not higher because of special privileges flowing from inadequate laws, inadequate regulations, and lax administration.

Let me outline five of the many justifications for an immediate moratorium on the granting of exemptions.

First, there is every indication that there have been laxness and irresponsibility in the supervision of foundations by the Internal Revenue Service. There is little doubt that the tremendous increase in the number and size of foundations has outrun the machinery for control. Moreover, a moratorium would give the Treasury Department an opportunity to tighten its exemption requirements, its supervisory procedure and control, and step up its disciplinary actions for violations of its regulations.

The scarcity of information on foundations and the lack of supervision has made it impossible for the Treasury to determine the extent of loss to the Federal Treasury on foundation operations. Commissioner Mortimer M. Caplin has advised me that he recognizes that his Department's "audit activity in the area of exempt organizations was inadequate in the past.". . .

The dearth of data without which neither the public, nor the Congress, nor the executive branch can properly evaluate the impact of the rapidly growing foundation industry is due, in part, to the deficiencies in administrative forms and procedures.

The law requires tax-exempt foundations to make a report of their operations on a tax return known as Form 990–A. This return is composed of four pages. It gives information concerning receipts, disbursements, and balance sheets. But Form 990–A omits vitally important facts. No report is required as to the date of contributions received or as to the type of contributions received—that is, whether it is cash, securities, real estate, etc. No information is required as to selling dates of assets. Notes receivable and accounts receivable are not separated. Mortgage holdings—a big foundation business—are not treated separately. Although a foundation is required to report 10 percent or more stock ownership, it is not required to report the date or manner of acquisition of the stock. No detail is required as to accounts payable, such as the nature of the accounts payable, name of the creditor, etc. Little detail is required as to the character of the items making up miscellaneous expenses. No description of the foundation's business activities is required. Names of the officers, directors, or trustees are not required.

Certainly, the stockholders of any business corporation would wish to have such information. And, in the case of tax-exempt foundations, the taxpayers are the stockholders since they provide the subsidy.

My second justification for urging a moratorium is that there appears to have been widespread disregard of Treasury regulations, despite penalties provided by law, including fines up to $10,000 and jail terms. Uneducated sharecroppers are presumed to know the law, but many of the foundations under study and their well-paid, well-educated advisers are apparently exempt from this ancient presumption, in practice, if not as a matter of strict law. Singling out the shortcomings of each individual foundation would fill countless pages so I shall only recite a few:

1. The Treasury Department requires every foundation to file the following information if it owns 10 percent or more of any class of stock of any corporation at the beginning or close of each reporting period: (1) Name of the corporation; (2) number of shares of each type of stock owned, including identification as to voting or nonvoting; and (3) the value of the stock as recorded on the foundation's books. We have already found 72 foundations, owning 10 percent or more of at least 1 class of stock in 1 or more of 180 different corporations during the years 1951 through 1960, who failed to report such information to the Internal Revenue Service for at least 1 year. . . .

The third justification for urging a moratorium relates to that provision of the Revenue Act of 1950 which prohibits "unreasonable" accumulations of income by foundations. The group of foundations we examined had accumulated income of $906,136,256 at the close of the last accounting period for which they submitted data to the committee (usually 1960), as against $271,615,733 at the close of the first accounting period (usually 1951) for which they provided information. The reasons for this huge increase in accumulated income will require further study. One of the problems is the failure of many foundations to report any information regarding their accumulated income. . . .

The fourth justification for urging a moratorium is that tax exemption for foundations needs reassessment in the light of the present times. There is every indication that many tax-exempt charitable foundations are being used for purposes not related to charity. The laws of the past are no longer effective. Congress could not envision the gigantic proportions that the foundation business would reach. During the last accounting period (usually 1960) for which the foundations submitted data to the committee, they had total receipts of $1,-034,710,518, as against total receipts of $554,740,568 during the first accounting period (usually 1951).

In 1960 there were 7,213,000 families, including unattached individuals, in the United States who had income of less than $2,000 before taxes. Their aggregate income was $8,040 million. Thus, the $1,034,710,518 received by the 534 tax-exempt foundations in 1960 was almost 13 percent of the income of 7,213,000 American families. In other words, the aggregate receipts of these 534 foundations were equal to that of 928,000 American families in 1960.

Moreover, the $1,034,710,518 received by the 534 tax-exempt foundations in 1960 was substantially more—in fact, almost 20 percent more—than the $864,435,000 combined net operating earnings, after taxes, of the 50 largest banks in the United States. . . .

What is the significance of the huge amounts accruing in the form of capital gains? The $1,477,272,841 income figure from capital gains suggests that many foundations have become a vehicle for trading in securities and dodging the capital gain tax. Foundation capital gains are not only tax exempt, but the foundations are permitted to place them in the principal account instead of the income account. . . .

This type of activity by foundations—with huge, untaxed funds at their disposal—poses some big questions in the light of the recent sharp breaks in the market. In my view, tax-exempt foundations—all of whom are supported by the taxpayers—should not be permitted to use public funds for speculation in the stock market. Their mistakes or misfortunes are too likely to have a disastrous effect on millions of our citizens.

The fifth justification for urging a moratorium is the need for achieving a more equitable distribution of the tax burden —one of the most pressing problems facing the Congress. In fairness to all taxpayers, the Congress should explore the foundation business as a possible new source of revenue.

Today funds are being put into foundations which yield no taxable income. Since the money lost to the public's Treasury must be found somewhere, the burden is shifted to people who are obliged to work for a living—to the widow with a cottage instead of a palace, to businessmen, and to the farmer.

In my view, it is extremely unfair for the taxpayers of the First District of Texas and the rest of the country to be compelled to pay for the maintenance of tax-exempt foundations. They mainly lighten the burden of wealthy people who do not require government subsidy. This is not backed by justice, equity, or sound American principles.

These five points are merely a summary statement of the justifications for urging an immediate moratorium on the creation of any more of these tax-exempt foundations until the Congress has taken appropriate action—but let me proceed with the report in more detail on the difficulties we have encountered, the evidences of the need for changes in the law, in the regulations, and in the administration of these organizations. . . .

In the past two decades numerous business organizations have become affiliated with or merged into so-called charitable foundations. As we all know, true charity has always been most favored in this great land of ours, and has been fostered by tax exemptions freely granted by our National, State, and local governments. However, when business organizations operate in the guise or cloak of charity primarily to evade taxes and to gain advantages over other business enterprises, it is time to carefully examine this field. Each tax exemption naturally increases the tax burden of the remainder of our citizens and businesses. If the burden of small business becomes too great, small businesses will fail and disappear, and our economy and system must likewise fail.

To date, our records disclose 111 foundations that owned 10 percent or more of at least 1 class of stock in 1 or more of 263 different corporations on December 31, 1960. . . . The companies are in a wide variety of industries: Rock and gravel, lime and cement, aluminum, textiles, railroads, broadcasting, real estate, retailing, including chainstores and department stores, soft drinks, railway equipment, chemicals, paper and paper products, stoves, oil and minerals, drugs, baking, cereals and other breakfast foods, sugar, banks, theaters, utilities, film and TV production, dies, arms, explosives, chemical research, ammunition, insurance, perfumes and cosmetics, shoes, refrigerators, construction, glass, tavern leasing, parking lots, heavy machinery, brewing, lead, coal, meatpacking, dress manufacturing, drugstores, hotels and motels, shopping centers, building materials and lumber, newspaper and other publishing, trucking and parcel delivery, wholesale plumbing and heating services, gasoline engines, compressors, refrigeration systems, manufacturing furriers, fiber cord, wooden barrels, and vulcanized fiber, among others.

The stock ownership of certain foundations under study ranges from 10 to 100 percent. . . .

Over the past year, my mail has brought renewed criticism

of the commercial activities of tax-exempt foundations. The American Council of Independent Laboratories, composed of about 150 independent, taxpaying research and testing laboratories, states that their competitors—tax-exempt research institutes—operate multi-million-dollar commercial businesses at a profit, and that they have grown tremendously at the expense of the taxpayer. It is alleged that seven of these tax-exempt organizations did over $100 million in research and testing business during 1959. . . .

Occasionally a foundation is found by the Internal Revenue Service to be engaging in an "unrelated business." This is not prohibited under the law, but the income from "unrelated business" is taxable.

On May 2, 1962, for example, the Internal Revenue Service held that the Educational Testing Service, of Princeton, N.J., a tax-exempt foundation since 1949, has been carrying on an unrelated business—selling tests and testing services to business, professional, and other non-educational customers. The income from these sales will be subject to tax from now on.

But the tax-exempt Honeywell Foundation, of Wabash, Ind., is permitted to operate a restaurant which is open to the public. . . .

As of December 31, 1960, the amount of money the Honeywell Foundation had invested in food service equipment was $109,377.57; the book amount was $52,188.79 after deducting the reserve for depreciation.

And the taxpaying competitor, of course, operates at a disadvantage. . . .

Although the IRS shies away from a detailed discussion of the subject, the evidence suggests the Service exercises only mild supervision over tax-exempt organizations.

The law requires some of the information on annual returns of the organizations to be available to the public—presumably to enable the public to assist the service in this supervision—but the IRS has chosen to interpret the mandate of law as narrowly as possible.

The public gets literally what the law requires—and no more. For example, every reporting organization must list "the total of the contributions and gifts received by it" each year for the Service and for the public. But the itemization of gifts exceeding $100, which the Service also demands, is closed from public scrutiny.

The Service insists on an itemization of contributions made by the organization, but says the public is entitled to know only the "classes" of contributions made.

The Service asks each organization annually whether it has engaged in political activity, but closes the reply from public view.

Seemingly overlooked in the law, and in IRS regulations, is the fact that exemption from income taxes and the power to collect deductible contributions is a tremendous privilege.

Complete disclosure of the activities of tax-exempt organizations could help insure that this privilege is not abused. . . .

It is hardly necessary to prove by statistical facts that business is becoming more and more concentrated—and, without a doubt, tax-exempt foundations are helping to push us in that direction.

There is every indication that foundation-controlled enterprises have unfair competitive advantages. This is so despite provisions of the present tax laws which deal with unrelated business income, sale and leaseback transactions, prohibited transactions, etc.

Some of these competitive advantages are as follows:

1. The "owner" of the foundation usually controls both the foundation and its business subsidiaries.

2. Readily available cash. It is quite an advantage to have a ready source for cash without having to assume a responsibility to banks or stockholders. On May 12, 1954, the Sears, Roebuck Foundation made a short-term loan in the amount of $1,200,000 at 3 percent interest to Sears, Roebuck & Co.

3. Foundation control of businesses puts taxpaying businessmen—particularly small businessmen—at the mercy of giants with tax umbrellas. A foundation-controlled business, with no stockholders to worry about could conceivably operate at a loss for some time in order to eliminate a competitor. It is suggested that in periods of recession destructive competition could result from foundation controlled enterprises since making a profit, paying dividends, and maintaining equity credit are of little concern to a privately controlled, tax-exempt foundation. . . .

The Internal Revenue Code contains no provision to prevent large funds from being built up by foundations from contributions received by them. Since a corporation's annual contribution to its foundation is capital in the hands of the foundation and only the income from these contributions need be distributed, the Internal Revenue Service cannot prevent large funds from being built up by corporation-created foundations. And, since contributions are not subject to the provisions for distribution annually, the prohibition against unreasonable accumulations does not apply.

Apparently, private individuals may even receive annuities from a foundation's income. The position of the Internal Revenue Service is that private individuals may not receive annuities from a foundation's income, but there are, however, court decisions which hold under the "predominant purpose" doctrine that the payment of annuities from a foundation's income does not preclude exemption. . . .

The following are among the subjects that need careful examination. They relate to the acquisition and use of foundation funds.

1. Foundations' business activities.

2. Foundations interlocked with a business through stock ownership and common control by the donor.

3. Foundations' moneylending activities. At present, the only restraint on moneylending of foundations appears to be that loans must carry a "reasonable" rate of interest. Commissioner Mortimer Caplin has advised me that a foundation or family trust may make a loan of corpus or income to the following persons, among others: "its creator, (2) his family, (3) the businesses under his control, or (4) a donor who has made a substantial contribution to the foundation. Generally, such a transaction would not constitute a basis for revocation of exemption." . . .

I am informed that, at the present time, so-called charitable foundations in certain States are created merely by a deed of trust. There is little adequate State or Federal regulation or supervision for the creation and administration of such organizations. In some States, foundations operate in secret since they do not register as nonprofit organizations under the provisions of applicable nonprofit codes. On the one hand, State authorities rely on the Internal Revenue Service to determine who is entitled to tax-exempt status. On the other hand, when an organization receives a nonprofit charter from the State, it carries considerable weight with the Internal Revenue Service. As a result, foundations are seldom properly scrutinized by any public authority. . . .

Apparently, some of our wealthier families are not content with just one tax-exempt foundation, and hence their foundations proliferate. So the "owners" have their main foundations, and then they have their subsidiary foundations.

For example, the Ford family has the Ford Foundation and then they have subsidiary foundations which include: Benson and Edith Ford Fund, Eleanor Clay Ford Fund, Henry and Anne Ford Fund, Walter and Josephine Ford Fund, William and Martha Ford Fund, and the Ford Motor Co. Fund. The total receipts, including contributions received, of the seven Ford foundations were $1,737,216,789 for the years 1951 through 1960; $1,670,207,470 of this amount applies to the Ford Foundation.

The Mellon family has the A.W. Educational & Charitable Trust as well as a number of subsidiaries which include the Richard King Mellon Foundation, Avalon Foundation, Bollingen Foundation, Sarah Mellon Scaife Foundation, and the Old Dominion Foundation. The total receipts, including contributions received, of the six Mellon foundations were $199,823,125 for the years 1951 through 1960.

The Rockefeller family has the Rockefeller Foundation as well as a number of subsidiary foundations which include China Medical Board of New York, Council on Economic and Cultural Affairs, American International Association for Economic and Social Development, Government Affairs Foundation of Albany, N.Y., Rockefeller Brothers Fund, Esso Education Foundation, General Education Board, Sealantic Fund, Inc., Colonial Williamsburg, the Rockefeller Institute, and Sleepy Hollow Restorations, Inc. The total receipts, including contributions received, of the 12 Rockefeller foundations were $660,706,900 for the years 1951 through

1960. $238,688,318 of this amount applies to the Rockefeller Foundation. . . .

Obviously, tax-exempt foundations have been and are being used, in part, to avoid Federal estate taxes. Thus huge fortunes are kept from being returned to public use for channeling into our economy without limitations.

The late Secretary of the Treasury Mellon used a charitable foundation to avoid estate taxes on a multimillion-dollar estate. Of more recent date, the Ford Foundation was used to reduce the taxable estates of Henry and Edsel Ford and to avoid having to sell Ford Motor Co. stock to the public in order to meet large estate taxes. Thus the Ford Foundation was given over 90 percent of the equity in the Ford Motor Co.

So substantial parts of the great fortunes of those who have profited by the enormous expansion of American industry have found their way into tax-exempt foundations. These foundations have already passed and will continue to pass—by right of inheritance—to the control of heirs or their trustees. This enables a few individuals to control ever increasing tax-exempt wealth.

Foundations today bear a frightening resemblance to the bank holding companies that were invented by the champions of monopoly and combination in the early 1900's. They characterized interlocking directorates and consolidations as "co-operation." At that time, some of our national banks were inseparably tied together with security holding companies in both ownership and management. These holding companies had unlimited powers—just as foundations do—to buy, sell, and speculate in stocks, just as if they were private investment corporations of boundless powers, with no public duties or responsibilities and not dependent on public confidence. Back in those days, the whole arrangement was merely a pretext behind which the bank's officers were merely shielding themselves in making money for the bank's stockholders through the prestige, resources, and organization of the bank—and by means that were forbidden to the bank.

The holding companies were so organized that their stock was always owned by the same person who owned the stock of the bank—and in the same proportions—while no person who was not a director of the bank could be a director of the holding company, and finally, the stock of the holding company had to be held by the officers of the bank as trustees. The bank and the holding company were thus one with the same association of persons—just as foundations and their "owners" and managers are one and inseparable.

Are we in fact witnessing today developments as destructive of genuine, healthy private enterprise as our predecessors were then?

It is evident that control of our industrial and commercial enterprises is to an ever-increasing degree passing into the hands of tax-exempt foundations through stock ownership. In my view, this is a dangerous situation with its boundless temptations and opportunities. I do not agree with the cheerful philosophy that the situation will right itself. The law must properly safeguard the community against possible abuses of the tax exemption privilege by the "owners" of foundations or their successors.

FOUNDATIONS AND THE GOVERNMENT: SOME OBSERVATIONS ON THE FUTURE *

by Mortimer M. Caplin

CONGRESSMAN PATMAN'S recent inquiries have once again turned the spotlight onto foundations and their place in our society. I need not rehearse his findings, both tentative and definite, except to indicate that, in his view, the Internal Revenue Service is not the proper agency to exercise truly effective supervisory control. This also happens to be my own view, if the kind of supervision and control exercised, for example, by the Securities and Exchange Commission over investment companies and public utility holding companies, should ever become necessary.

Public attention has, however, been directed toward foundations, with a strongly issued invitation that a long, close look be taken. How does the Revenue Service fit into this developing picture? I think it fair to say that before 1961, certainly, our audit pattern was rather heavily oriented toward the "most productive" situations—i.e. toward an examination of those tax returns where deficiencies seemed most likely. This was a

* "Foundations and the Government: Some Observations on the Future," *Foundation News*, 4 (May, 1963), 1–3. Mortimer M. Caplin was Commissioner of Internal Revenue from 1961 to 1964. He practices law in Washington, D.C.

rather short-sighted approach. Of the more than $99 billion collected in taxes last year, fully 97% was either voluntary or pre-collected as withholding. No country in the world can match such a record of compliance—it is truly the heart of our taxing system. Taking the longer view, I concluded, shortly after becoming Commissioner, that what was most needed, and what the Revenue Service could most usefully help to accomplish, was a further strengthening of public confidence in our taxing system. By looking into areas of abuse, and of potential abuse, we seek to build public confidence in the overall fairness of American taxation and establish in the public mind a sense of administration without favoritism, across the board.

Accordingly, the Revenue Service has modified its audit pattern. We are examining much more heavily in areas which may indeed produce no deficiencies, and thus no revenue for the government, because we feel that the public at large needs assurance that everyone is being checked into—and on some reasonable cyclical basis. I am, of course, referring to more than foundations alone: all tax-exempt organizations are covered in the expanded audit program.

What have we found, enquiring into foundation practices? There have been abuses. We have found self-dealing between the foundation and insider groups; some losses of exemption have resulted. We have found unreasonable accumulations. We have found speculative investments—such things as third mortgages on Florida real estate and the so-called "ABC" oil transactions. We have found foundations actually going out and competing for interest income, and for rental income. We have even found manipulation of leases, with the obvious purpose of evading the "business lease" provisions of the tax laws, applicable to certain leases of at least five years in duration. In short, we have found a wide variety of transactions close to, as well as on the other side of, legality—violations of the spirit, if not always of the letter, of the law. Congressman Patman's investigations have been of considerable assistance—and impetus—to us, in these matters. . . .

I have every hope that harsh corrective legislation will not be necessary. One wholesome substitute would be an effective program of self-policing by foundations. Other tax-exempt groups have already begun such programs. The college fund-raisers, for example, have been much concerned about certain abuses occurring within their ranks. After holding meetings on the subject, they are pressing for effective measures of self-policing. Studies are under way—in which, let me point out, the Revenue Service is cooperating—and experienced consultants are to be hired. Art museums and art associations have also been disturbed by abuses arising from over-valuation of donated art objects, and will take steps to correct them. So too, will dealers in rare manuscripts. And so on.

Legislation now on the books provides a good deal of room for more vigorous enforcement on our part. We intend to be vigorous; we have the responsibility to be. But the foundations can, as I say, do a great deal to help both us and themselves. I would suggest five courses of action:

(1) Foundations should strive to foster public trust in their operations. I am not thinking so much of mere publicity as I am of disclosure and of an awareness that public trust is something to be avidly sought. Foundations should both act and speak in a manner which recognizes that they have been charged with a public trust and are obligated to live up to it.

(2) Foundations should not simply obey the law—or, rather, they should not confine themselves to avoiding its penalties. Borderline transactions, strictly legal perhaps, but in

spirit running distinctly against the statutory grain, should be as carefully shunned as are clearly proscribed transactions. In other words, foundations should strive to understand and co-operate with the law, rather than to outwit or to take advantage of it.

(3) Foundations should file information returns with the federal (and where required the state) government which are in all respects unexceptionable—clear, complete, accurate, and timely. Few things are more basic to public trust than public knowledge.

(4) When the Revenue Service initiates audit procedures, foundations should cooperate to the fullest extent possible. The Service should not be thought of as alien or inimical to foundation operations. Both sides have their jobs to do; both sides should endeavor to fulfill all obligations in an atmosphere of mutual respect and understanding.

(5) Foundations should give serious thought to the formulation of a specific code of conduct. I am not proposing a trade association, or the merging of individual identities into some sort of semi-collective entity. But the precise standards which foundations should observe, in commonly experienced situations, have yet to be articulated. It seems to me desirable that the foundations themselves make—and then observe—such a formulation. I believe that such a recognized code would be a giant step forward in establishing the kind of meaningful program of self-policing I am advocating.

The promotion of private philanthropy through tax forgiveness is a basic tenet of the United States tax system. That basic tenet is not threatened by the President's current tax proposals, nor is it endangered by the Revenue Service's current enforcement program. What could cause serious and untoward developments, it seems to me, would be the failure of the foundations themselves to live up to their role—the role envisaged for them by the spirit of our tax laws and increasingly insisted upon by the American public.

TREASURY DEPARTMENT REPORT ON PRIVATE FOUNDATIONS *

THE TREASURY DEPARTMENT's study of private foundations has revealed the existence of six categories of major problems.

A. Self-Dealing

Some donors who create or make substantial contributions to a private foundation have engaged in other transactions with the foundation. Property may be rented to or from it; assets may be sold to it or purchased from it; money may be borrowed from it or loaned to it. These transactions are rarely necessary to the discharge of the foundation's charitable objectives; and they give rise to very real danger of diversion of foundation assets to private advantage.

Cognizant of this danger, the House of Representatives in 1950 approved a bill which would have imposed absolute prohibitions upon most financial intercourse between foundations and donors or related parties, and which would have severely restricted other such dealings. However, the measure finally adopted, which has been carried without material change into

---

* Committee on Finance, United States Senate, *Treasury Department Report on Private Foundations* (Washington, D.C.: U.S. Government Printing Office, 1965), pp. 6–10. This report was published with the purpose of providing information to the Senate Committee on Finance.

present law, prohibits only loans which do not bear a "reasonable" rate of interest and do not have "adequate" security, "substantial" purchases of property for more than "adequate" consideration, and certain other transactions.

Fourteen years of experience have demonstrated that the imprecision of this statute makes the law difficult and expensive to administer, hard to enforce in litigation, and otherwise insufficient to prevent abuses. Whatever minor advantages charity may occasionally derive from the opportunity for free dealings between foundations and donors are too slight to overcome the weight of these considerations. Consequently, the Report recommends legislative rules patterned on the total prohibitions of the 1950 House bill. The effect of this recommendation would, generally, be to prevent private foundations from dealing with any substantial contributor, any officer, director, or trustee of the foundation, or any party related to them, except to pay reasonable compensation for necessary services and to make incidental purchases of supplies.

B. Delay in Benefit to Charity

The tax laws grant current deductions for charitable contributions upon the assumption that the funds will benefit the public welfare. This aim can be thwarted when the benefits are too long delayed. Typically, contributions to a foundation are retained as capital, rather than distributed. While this procedure is justified by the advantages which private foundations can bring to our society, in few situations is there justification for the retention of income (except long-term capital gains) by foundations over extended periods. Similarly, the purposes of charity are not well served when a foundation's charitable disbursements are restricted by the investment of its funds in assets which produce little or no current income.

Taking note of the disadvantages to charity of permitting unrestricted accumulations of income, Congress in 1950 enacted the predecessor of section 504 of the present Internal Revenue Code, which denies an organization's exemption for any year in which its income accumulations are (a) "unreasonable" in amount or duration for accomplishing its exempt purposes, (b) used to a "substantial" degree for other purposes, or (c) invested in a way which "jeopardizes" the achievement of its charitable objectives.[1] The indefiniteness of the section's standards, however, has rendered this provision difficult to apply and even more difficult to enforce. Two changes in the law are needed for private foundations which do not carry on substantial active charitable endeavors of their own.

First, such private foundations should be required to devote all of their net income[2] to active charitable operations (whether conducted by themselves or by other charitable organizations) on a reasonably current basis. To afford flexibility, the requirements should be tempered by a 5-year carryforward provision and a rule permitting accumulation for a specified reasonable period if their purpose is clearly designated in advance and accumulation by the foundation is necessary to that purpose.

Second, in the case of nonoperating private foundations which minimize their regular income by concentrating their investments in low yielding assets, an "income equivalent" formula should be provided to place them on a parity with

---

[1] Section 681 imposes similar restrictions upon nonexempt trusts which, under section 642 (c), claim charitable deductions in excess of the ordinary percentage limitations on individuals' deductible contributions.

[2] Except long-term capital gains [also applies next page, line 3].

foundations having more diversified portfolios. This result can be accomplished by requiring that they disburse an amount equal either to actual foundation net income [2] or to a fixed percentage of foundation asset value, whichever is greater.

C. *Foundation Involvement in Business*

Many private foundations have become deeply involved in the active conduct of business enterprises. Ordinarily, the involvement takes the form of ownership of a controlling interest in one or more corporations which operate businesses; occasionally, a foundation owns and operates a business directly. Interests which do not constitute control may nonetheless be of sufficient magnitude to produce involvement in the affairs of the business.

Serious difficulties result from foundation commitment to business endeavors. Regular business enterprises may suffer serious competitive disadvantage. Moreover, opportunities and temptations for subtle and varied forms of self-dealing—difficult to detect and impossible completely to proscribe—proliferate. Foundation management may be drawn from concern with charitable activities to time-consuming concentration on the affairs and problems of the commercial enterprise.

For these reasons, the Report proposes the imposition of an absolute limit upon the participation of private foundations in active business, whether presently owned or subsequently acquired. This recommendation would prohibit a foundation from owning, either directly or through stock holdings, 20 percent or more of a business unrelated to the charitable activities of the foundation. . . . Foundations would be granted a prescribed reasonable period, subject to extension, in which to reduce their present or subsequently acquired business interests below the specified maximum limit.

D. *Family Use of Foundations to Control Corporate and Other Property*

Donors have frequently transferred to private foundations stock of corporations over which the donor maintains control. The resulting relationships among the foundation, corporation, and donor have serious undesirable consequences which require correction. Similar problems arise when a donor contributes an interest in an unincorporated business, or an undivided interest in property, in which he or related parties continue to have substantial rights. In all of these situations, there is substantial likelihood that private interests will be preferred at the expense of charity. Indeed, each of the three major abuses discussed thus far may be presented in acute form here. The problems here are sufficiently intensified, complex, and possessed of novel ramifications to require a special remedy.

To provide such a remedy, the Treasury Department recommends the adoption of legislation which, for gifts made in the future, would recognize that the transfer of an interest in a family corporation or other controlled property lacks the finality which should characterize a deductible charitable contribution. Under this recommendation, where the donor and related parties maintain control of a business or other property after the contribution of an interest in it to a private foundation, no income tax deduction would be permitted for the gift until (a) the foundation disposes of the contributed asset, (b) the foundation devotes the property to active charitable operations, or (c) donor control over the business or property terminates. Correlatively, the recommended legislation would treat transfers of such interests, made at or before death, as incomplete for all estate tax purposes unless one of the three qualifying events occurs within a specified period (subject to limited extension) after the donor's death. For the purposes of this rule, control would be presumed to exist if the donor and related parties own 20 percent of the voting power of a corporation or a 20 percent interest in an unincorporated business or other property. This presumption could be rebutted by a showing that a particular interest does not constitute control. In determining whether or not the donor and related parties possess control, interests held by the foundation would be attributed to them until all of their own rights in the business or other underlying property cease.

The Treasury Department has given careful consideration to a modification of this proposal which would postpone the donor's deduction only where, after the contribution, he and related parties control the business or other underlying property and, in addition, exercise substantial influence upon the foundation to which the contribution was made. Such a rule would permit an immediate deduction to a donor who transfers controlled property to a foundation over which he does not have substantial influence. Analysis of this modification indicates that it possesses both advantages and disadvantages. Congressional evaluation of the matter, hence, will require careful balancing of the two.

E. Financial Transactions Unrelated to Charitable Functions

Private foundations necessarily engage in many financial transactions connected with the investment of their funds. Experience has, however, indicated that unrestricted foundation participation in three classes of financial activities which are not essential to charitable operations or investment programs can produce seriously unfortunate results.

Some foundations have borrowed heavily to acquire productive assets. In doing so, they have often permitted diversions of a portion of the benefit of their tax exemptions to private parties, and they have been able to swell their holdings markedly without dependence upon contributors. Certain foundations have made loans whose fundamental motivation was the creation of unwarranted private advantage. The borrowers, however, were beyond the scope of reasonable and administrable prohibitions on foundation self-dealing, and the benefits accruing to the foundation's managers or donors were sufficiently nebulous and removed from the loan transactions themselves to be difficult to discover, identify, and prove. Some foundations have participated in active trading of securities or speculative practices.

The Treasury Department recommends special rules to deal with each of these three classes of unrelated financial transactions. First, it proposes that all borrowing by private foundations for investment purposes be prohibited.[3] Second, it recommends that foundation loans be confined to categories which are clearly necessary, safe, and appropriate for charitable fiduciaries. Third, it proposes that foundations be prohibited from trading activities and speculative practices.

F. Broadening of Foundation Management

Present law imposes no limit upon the period of time during which a donor or his family may exercise substantial influence upon the affairs of a private foundation. While close donor involvement with a foundation during its early years can provide unique direction for the foundation's activities and infuse spirit and enthusiasm into its charitable endeavors, these ef-

[3] This recommendation would not prevent foundations from borrowing money to carry on their exempt functions.

fects tend to diminish with the passage of time, and are likely to disappear altogether with the donor's death. On the other hand, influence by a donor or his family presents opportunities for private advantage and public detriment which are too subtle and refined for specific prohibitions to prevent; it provides no assurance that the foundation will receive objective evaluation by private parties who can terminate the organization if, after a reasonable period of time, it has not proved itself; and it permits the development of narrowness of view and inflexibility in foundation management. Consequently, the Treasury Department recommends an approach which would broaden the base of foundation management after the first 25 years of the foundation's life. Under this proposal, the donor and related parties would not be permitted to constitute more than 25 percent of the foundation's governing body after the expiration of the prescribed period of time. Foundations which have now been in existence for 25 years would be permitted to continue subject to substantial donor influence for a period of from 5 to 10 years from the present time. [Four brief, more technical suggestions follow.]

These Treasury Department proposals are based upon a recognition that private foundations can and do make a major contribution to our society. The proposals have been carefully devised to eliminate subordination of charitable interests to personal interests, to stimulate the flow of foundation funds to active, useful programs, and to focus the energies of foundation fiduciaries upon their philanthropic functions. The recommendations seek not only to end diversions, distractions, and abuses, but to stimulate and foster the active pursuit of charitable ends which the tax laws seek to encourage. Any restraints which the proposals may impose on the flow of funds to private foundations will be far outweighed by the benefits which will accrue to charity from the removal of abuses and from the elimination of the shadow which the existence of abuse now casts upon the private foundation area.

VIEWS OF THE
TREASURY REPORT *

THE TREASURY DEPARTMENT Report on Private Foundations issued in February, 1965, discussed and proposed remedies for "six categories of major problems" in the foundation field, and some minor ones. This memorandum makes brief observations, in nonlegal language, on these six items. It does not present, except as occasional illustration, special aspects which might affect a small number of foundations. Details of this sort are available almost *ad infinitum* in the 771 pages of the two-volume *Written Statements of Interested Individuals and Organizations.* . . .

As the Treasury itself reported, "the preponderant number of private foundations perform their functions without tax abuse," and few of the proposals, if enacted into law, would require substantial changes in the grant-making or investment practices of most foundations. The Report itself is in the main judicious and factual, and the effort to correct abuses praiseworthy. What mainly needs closer examination are the side

* "Views of the Treasury Report," prepared by the staff of the Russell Sage Foundation in consultation with F. Emerson Andrews, *Foundation News,* 9 (March, 1968), 29–33.

effects of some of these proposals, not merely upon existing legitimate foundations, but upon the total flow of philanthropic funds.

Before individual proposals are discussed, a general question that applies to nearly all the proposals should be examined. Should controlling legislation and supervising agencies be at the federal or the state level?

Since most foundations, whether corporations or trusts, are creations under state law, a presumption exists that registration, reporting, and supervision should be primarily a state function, with enforcement by the state attorneys general. Indeed, at the federal level the Internal Revenue Service has only a singularly inappropriate sanction, the denial of exempt status. For some infractions, however clearly proved, this is too severe, and therefore not apt to be applied. For others, it is inappropriate, for it does not extend to removing, or making personally liable, errant trustees, and results usually in reducing, not expanding, benefits to the intended charitable recipients.

But whatever the logic of the situation, presently only eleven states (New York was added on January 1, 1967) have any substantial legislation requiring registration and reporting, and in many of these states this legislation affects only trusts, or actual administration is not now effective. Though with the addition of New York State to this group a substantial percentage of all foundations will be in reporting states, serious gaps and inadequacies may continue for many years at the state level.

In any event an Administration bill based on the Treasury proposals is anticipated in the near future. It needs to be discussed at the federal level, but the state alternative should be considered with respect to some of the proposals.

186

1. Self-Dealing

The Treasury proposes absolute prohibitions upon most financial transactions between foundations and the donor or related parties. The present law, passed in 1950, prohibits most such transactions unless carried on at arm's length, or at a "reasonable" rate of interest, with "adequate" security, and the like. The Treasury reports that after fifteen years of administrative experience it has found the "prohibited transactions" section almost impossible to enforce; first, because of inability to audit foundation reports with enough thoroughness to discover most of the infractions, and, second, because of varying court interpretations of "reasonable," "adequate," and the like.

The proposal for absolute prohibition seems unobjectionable, if provision is made for prompt review and exceptions in certain hardship situations. For example, The Ford Foundation presently owns a large block of Ford Motor Company nonvoting stock. In the past the Company has been willing to exchange portions of this nonvoting stock for voting stock, which the Foundation could then exchange or sell. This degree of self-dealing would seem unobjectionable. But it would not be appropriate to permit continuance of a present practice common in Louisiana and Texas whereby a person or company sells to a related foundation buildings or land, receiving only notes on the property itself for security, then rents back the property, and thereby avoids certain local taxes which are assessed on equity interests in real property.

2. Delay in Benefit to Charity

The Treasury proposes that grant-making foundations be required to spend their investment income within the year of receipt or the year following. Further, if investments are in assets yielding low or no income, the foundation would be required to invade capital, if this is necessary, in order to pay out an amount representing a reasonable return (averaged college portfolios are mentioned as a measure) from market value of assets at the beginning of the fiscal year.

The Treasury's position seems in general sound. The 1950 revision of the Code had been intended to accomplish this objective with its provision for loss of exemption in cases of "unreasonable" accumulations, but "unreasonable" has never been adequately defined, and the courts have been wayward in their rulings. A few matters of definition need to be explored.

"Assets at market value" may present problems of valuation. Also, a foundation may be given a nonincome producing asset, for example, a painting. In another section the Treasury proposes that such gifts (unless, of course, the foundation operated a museum so that the gift is of public use) be not deductible as contributions until sold by the foundation and thus translated into an income-producing asset. Nearly the same result might be achieved by requiring that the gift be valued at the amount claimed in the original charitable deduction, and income at the agreed per cent be expended from other revenue or capital.

"Income" is acceptably defined as investment-type income, not including capital gains. Indeed, one extreme form of "capital gain" might deserve modification: the depletion allowance is permitting benefiting foundations to build up capital at an extremely rapid rate.

The Treasury proposes to treat as actual expenditure amounts set aside for a definite charitable purpose where the purpose requires accumulation for its accomplishment, with such sums to be expended within a specified period, such as not more than five years. This is a reasonable and necessary exception.

The term of one year after receipt is too short. Foundations which receive sudden large increases in income, as upon the death of a wealthy donor, need more time to devise constructive programs. A provision for both carry-forward and carry-back over a period of three years would be workable, and still achieve the Treasury objectives.

The present drastic sanction of loss of exempt status for infractions is both too severe and inappropriate. The penalty might better be corporate (or in the case of trusts, individual) income tax on the accumulated income.

3. Foundation Involvement in Business

The Treasury reports that many foundations are deeply involved in the active conduct of business enterprises, and that both problems and serious abuses frequently arise from such involvement. It proposes prohibiting a foundation from owning directly or through stock holdings, 20 per cent or more of a business unrelated to its charitable activities. A reasonable period would be allowed for reduction of present or subsequently acquired business interests exceeding this limit.

The problems are real and numerous. The 1950 Revenue Act taxed at ordinary corporation rates the income from unrelated business, but means of evasion have been discovered, and this provision does not correct all sources of abuse. At an extreme a donor may contribute stock of a closely held corporation to his foundation, taking his deduction at a value determined by perhaps a single sale arranged by himself, continue to vote the contributed stock, and with this control vote handsome salaries to family members employed in the controlled company, and declare little or no dividends, so that the charity has negligible income.

Close to the other end of the spectrum are a substantial number of very large foundations whose assets are chiefly the common stock of the donor's company, sometimes amounting to effective voting control. In most of these cases regular dividends are voted, and a recent study indicates that the investment return is often better than a diversified portfolio would yield. Here no abuse is presently apparent, but a conflict of interest may arise. If at a later date the stock became less desirable, would the trustees, probably family members or otherwise related to the company, be able to take the possibly drastic action required by the charity's interest?

With reference to this proposed adjustment, and in both greater and less degree in connection with the other proposals, consideration needs to be given to possible effect on total flow of philanthropic funds. Without the stimulus of the convenience, and sometimes personal advantages, of the given arrangement, would the gift be made at all? Where is the social balance for restrictions that would indeed prevent some abuses, but also severely reduce total contributions, many of which involve no abuse?

If such side effects are not deemed serious, the Treasury's 20 per cent proposal seems feasible, provided ample time is given for required diversification, with a possibility of exceptions being made for assets for which no ready outside market exists. Separate legislation has already been proposed to correct the "bootstrap" operation involved in the Brown decision.

4. Family Use of Foundations to Control Corporate and Other Property

The Treasury reports that foundations have frequently been established primarily to maintain control of a private corporation within the family while diminishing the burden of income, gift, and estate taxes. This may be done through contributing voting stock to a controlled foundation, thus avoiding estate tax, and this stock can be voted by younger members of the family to whom control of the foundation is transferred. Or it can be accomplished through gifts of non-voting stock, which permits transfer of effective control through gift of a small amount of voting stock. Various abuses result, in some respects differing little from those noted under Item 3.

The Treasury recommends that such transfers of an interest in a family corporation or other controlled property be not recognized for charitable deduction until the foundation disposes of the contributed asset, or devotes it to an active charitable operation, or donor control over the business or property terminates. Unlike the "involvement in business" rule where 20 per cent ownership by the foundation is the measure of control, this regulation would apply wherever the total interest of foundation, donor, and related parties constitute control.

There would be an obvious overlap in many cases between proposals 3 and 4, and the separate proposals under 4 are probably not necessary. With a limitation to less than 20 per cent of the stock of any corporation, a limit is placed on amount of stock transfer. If the foundation-and-donor controlled corporation failed to pay reasonable dividends, payment in some form would be required under the "delay in benefit" provisions in Section 2. Gross self-dealing would be prevented by the tighter restrictions of Section 1 and even the existing Prohibited Transactions section.

Withholding deductibility on gifts of stock in a controlled corporation would present major difficulties for donors who may have little else to give. Several large and effective foundations could be mentioned which probably would not be in existence today had this proposal been in effect.

5. Financial Transactions Unrelated to Charitable Functions

The Treasury proposes restrictions or prohibitions on three types of financial transactions in which some foundations presently indulge. It would prohibit all borrowing by private foundations for investment purposes. It recommends that loans be confined to categories clearly safe and appropriate for charitable fiduciaries. It would prohibit extensive trading activities and speculative practices.

Under suitable definition, all of these proposals seem reasonable. A foundation may sometimes need to borrow against future income to finance an urgent project, but to borrow for investment usually means an attempt to trade upon its tax exemption in behalf of its donor or some other interest. Loans for proper and legitimate investment, or program-type loans for needy students or low-cost housing, are proper, but what the Treasury calls "privately motivated" lending is not. Prudent investment management, particularly for a large foundation, may involve substantial portfolio changes from time to time. But frequent trading with a view to short-term speculative profit is not a proper function.

6. Broadening of Foundation Management

The Treasury Department views with concern the lack of any limit upon the time during which a donor or his family may substantially influence a private foundation. However, it rejects a proposal sometimes made, for an absolute limit upon the life of foundations, sometimes set at 25 years. It proposes that the donor and related parties be not permitted to constitute more than 25 per cent of the foundation's governing body after 25 years, with a five or ten year adjustment period with respect to foundations already of that age.

It is not easy to see how a question of this sort, primarily sociological and philosophical, should fall within the proposed control of a tax-gathering agency. However, the proposal has been made, and should be examined.

For one large class of foundations, those "sponsored" by companies and devoted to facilitating corporation giving, this proposal is inappropriate and may be death-dealing. Presently the trustees of these foundations are predominantly, and sometimes wholly, officers and directors of the parent company. They do not operate on income from endowment, but primarily from current gifts of the sponsoring company. While the courts have generously interpreted the rights of business corporations to make donations, it still remains true that they may not use stockholder money without at least a tenuous relation to the benefit of the corporation, its stockholders, employees, or its business relationships. It is probable that a company could not legally contribute undirected funds to an organization under majority control of persons legally required to have no relation to the company.

In the case of some family foundations the primary intent appears to be a regularization of family giving, with enrichment from experience and perhaps some professional guidance. Younger members of the family are brought into this continuing process. While outside persons may bring added perspective, so long as the foundation remains primarily a channel for current giving, it is not likely that the family members would be willing to surrender substantial control.

On the other hand, the multiplication of small perpetuities that never can afford professional guidance and may not offer enough income to interest trustees after the donor's death, do present a growing problem in America. But the Treasury proposal for broadening boards does not solve this problem, and may further complicate it. A requirement for either spending out capital or amalgamation in such organizations as community foundations may become desirable, but this is not the present proposal.

Most of the larger, older foundations have in fact moved away from family control and predominantly family membership over the years. The Treasury proposal may prove unnecessary in the light of longer experience, and in many respects seems unwise.

And, Finally—

The Treasury has presented a *Report* that is in all respects worthy of serious consideration. It presents evidence of severe abuses, and though these are limited to a fraction of foundations, mostly small, efforts to prevent and correct these abuses should be made.

One overriding difficulty remains. The regulatory proposals appear to be limited to private foundations. No mention is made of application of the same regulations, where pertinent, to other portions of the exempt field, such as colleges, hospitals, churches.

It usually will not be possible to correct an abuse unless the corrective measures apply generally. When unrelated businesses were taxed to foundations, the churches moved massively in. If a donor can no longer give stock of his closely held corporation to his foundation, will he not readily find a cooperative small college, local hospital, or private school? In New York State, after restrictive legislation on fund raising was passed some years ago, it was said that "Religion is becoming the last refuge of the charity racketeer."

It is recognized that broadening the regulatory effort to the whole charity field may, at least for some proposals, prove politically not feasible. But without such broadening the measures may do no more than transfer abuses they were intended to cure.

THE FREE-WHEELING
FOUNDATIONS *

by Wright Patman

As THE tax-exempt foundations have grown and proliferated, abuses of their privileged status have also grown, to the point that concerns the American taxpayer. Our investigations have demonstrated a serious need to enforce more strictly existing statutes governing the financial affairs of foundations, and to enact new legislation enabling the Government to regulate them more nearly in the public interest.

The present economy makes rising demands on the tax-

* "The Free-Wheeling Foundations," *The Progressive*, 31 (June, 1967), 27–31.

payer for both external defense and internal improvements, yet the privileged foundations do not share the tax pinch. Their increased hoarding and building of untaxed wealth makes warnings such as expressed by Senator Albert Gore of Tennessee—that the proliferation of tax-exempt foundations raises the threat of a dangerous "concentration of wealth and control over the economy"—sound indeed temperate.

The aggregate receipts of the 575 foundations under study by the House Small Business Subcommittee on Foundations have increased sharply since the 1950's. During the four years 1961 through 1964, they took in $4.6 billion compared with receipts of $6.9 billion during the preceding ten years, 1951 through 1960. At the pace they are scrambling for profits in the Sixties, their receipts will outdo those of the 1950's by one hundred per cent.

These are impressive, and disquieting, achievements. The receipts of these foundations for 1961 through 1964 were nearly thirty per cent higher than the combined net operating earnings—$3.6 billion after taxes—of the fifty largest banks in the United States.

How great a share of the receipts of some of these foundations came from the Central Intelligence Agency probably will never be known to the public, or even to most members of the Congress. But the CIA undoubtedly conveyed millions of dollars of the taxpayers' money through foundation pipelines to organizations and individuals in this country and overseas that the CIA counted on to support the agency's objectives.

One of the principal reasons for the mushrooming of foundation funds is the great tax privileges they enjoy. According to the pliable laws that supposedly regulate foundations, capital gains, for example, not only escape taxation but they also do not have to be given to charitable or educational causes if they are reinvested within a reasonable period of time. Many foundation executives spend a great deal of time jockeying their assets by trading in their stock market. The effect of this privileged gaming with stocks is, of course, that sometimes the foundations lose. But they care little about that since they are, in effect, using the public's money for stakes.

By and large, the 575 foundations covered in our subcommittee study have done very well in their market play. During the four years 1961 through 1964, they had capital gains (mostly from stock market transactions) of $1.3 billion—compared to the capital gains of $1.4 billion which it took these foundations ten years—1951 through 1960—to accumulate.

Here is a huge amount of income, this capital gains harvest, which should be distributed on a reasonably current basis. The pressure of the country's antipoverty needs, the nation's health needs, the nation's education, research, and scientific needs, and all other worthwhile causes demand that Congress force the distribution of these funds by law.

Tax laws and Treasury regulations invite, however, the use of capital gains in more selfish ways. The accountability demanded of foundations is weighted in their favor. For example, during a given year a foundation had dividends of $50,-000, capital gains of $10,000, which were reinvested within a reasonable period of time, and cash contributions received of $5,000—for total receipts of $65,000. It had no expenses and made grants totaling $35,000. This leaves the foundation $30,000 ahead, but as matters stand today, neither the $10,000 capital gains nor the $5,000 contributions received would be counted by the Treasury as accumulated income. The foundation could pretend that it was only $15,000 ahead. The other half of the $30,000 would just disappear from public view. This is happening all the time, by the millions of dollars and with the Treasury's blessing.

The generosity of the Federal Government goes further: It not only fails to require foundations to disburse capital gains if they are reinvested within a reasonable period of time, but it also gives them credit for capital losses. The law says that a foundation shall not have an unreasonable accumulation of income. For purposes of determining the amount of income accumulated by a foundation during a year, the Treasury excludes from income capital gains and contributions received. However, strangely enough, capital losses are deducted from income in such determinations. Thus, the coin has only one face and the foundations cannot help but win.

The permissive anarchy that surrounds the foundations' use of their capital gains is not unique; the Treasury has advised the Small Business Subcommittee that its interpretation of the law makes permissive the foundations' speculations even with dividends or interest—that the Treasury is, in short, perfectly willing for the foundations to reinvest and speculate with income which most normal interpretations of the law would seem to restrict specifically to educational and charitable expenditures.

One reason for the Treasury's tolerance may be found in the fact that it has established other regulations which make it extremely difficult to police foundation expenditures. One of the oddest of the Treasury oddities is that it does not require foundations to maintain separate accounts for income and principal; both can be thrown into the same bag, shaken up, mixed, and confused until it is impossible to separate income from principal funds. Hence, the setup is uniquely favorable to a foundation's profiteering by obtaining non-distributable capital gains through investing income which was supposed to have been distributed. For instance, under present Treasury opinion, a foundation could receive a $100,000 dividend and immediately invest the funds in stock instead of giving it to the causes the foundation is designed to aid.

The crediting of speculative losses to a foundation's books in the same way that grants are credited can only encourage wildcat investments. Investments should be made rigorously subject to whatever statutory rules are needed to protect the public's interest in the assets of foundations. The Ford Foundation and the Helen Hay Whitney Foundation of New York City were among the "sophisticated investors" caught in the collapse of the Atlantic Acceptance Corporation of Canada in 1965—Canada's biggest financial failure. The Ford Foundation may lose $6.7 million and the Helen Hay Whitney Foundation $338,400.

If these were the most spectacular, they were far from being the only losses incurred by foundations in recent years. To cite a few: The Josephine E. Gordon Foundation of Detroit experienced a 1964 capital loss of nearly $3.9 million. The 1962 capital loss of the Alfred P. Sloan Foundation of New York was $1,147,789, and the J. M. Kaplan Fund of New York reported a 1962 loss of $968,910.

The conscience of Congress surely must attend promptly to reforms that will make it impossible for these and other tax-free leviathans to engage in speculations with money that should go to help the causes for which the foundations were created.

The 575 Foundations studied by the Subcommittee claimed they paid out $2.2 billion in gifts, grants, scholarships, and other expenditures during the four-year period 1961 through 1964. But even this amount—which is only forty-eight per cent of their receipts—is probably inflated, for many foundations report "appropriations" instead of actual payments, and later, losing interest in certain projects, cancel all or part of the appropriated funds. In the preceding ten years—1951 through 1960—these foundations claimed similar disbursements totaling $3.3 billion or forty-eight per cent of total receipts.

The foundations develop a highly-structured and well-paid bureaucracy of their own. Because of the existence of this desk army, sizable foundation funds go into "expenses." Expenses claimed by the 575 foundations, including administrative and operating expenses, totaled $499,959,711 during the four-year period embraced by this study—more than ten per cent of the total receipts. During the decade 1951 through 1960, $742 million—roughly ten per cent of the total receipts —went into expenses. As an example of the generosity of foundations with trustees, there is the Alexander & Margaret Stewart Trust of Washington, D. C. Between 1961 and 1964, its annual charitable disbursements ranged from $244,000 to $283,000. The three trustees—George F. Hamilton, L. W. Holbrook, and the Union Trust Company—collected "commissions" in the aggregate amount of $40,000 to $43,000 annually, or somewhat more than fifteen per cent of the total annual disbursements for charitable causes.

Another case of the way incidentals sponge up the charitable content was found in the experience of the American Box Board Company Foundation of Grand Rapids, Michigan, which had gross income of $31,635 during its fiscal year 1964 but could do no good with it because "expenses" of $31,268 —including "miscellaneous expenses" of $24,452—ate it up. How does a foundation run up $31,268 in expenses fulfilling none of the espoused goals in its charter? This is one of the considerable and recurring mysteries that surround some foundations.

The foundations of America, which as a whole make up one of the most powerful economic and propaganda forces in modern times, are virtually unregulated. U.S. Treasury officials have not done an effective job of refereeing their operations; much less have they disturbed the foundations with some hard inquiries into investments and expenditures.

The Treasury does not yet even know how many foundations there are. More than two and one half years ago, on July 21, 1964, then Secretary Douglas Dillon testified before our Subcommittee:

"The Chairman is quite right in saying that the Treasury does not know how many foundations there are. Because of the growth of this area, I think that is knowledge that we should have, and we are in the process of acquiring it. . . . Now, with the advent of electronic data equipment the Internal Revenue Service is in the process of asking all exempt organizations, which are many hundreds of thousands, for statistical information which will enable classification into foundations, fraternal orders, religious orders, or whatever it is, and they intend to put all this information on a master electronic tape which will be kept up to date currently so we will have that information. But that will not be completed for about a year."

Now the third year is rounding out, and we still have not received this information from the Treasury.

During our hearings, when Secretary Dillon was asked, 'Would you agree that there are an infinite number of ways in which foundation assets or income can be used for the preferment of one set of private persons over another?" he answered, "I assume there are all sorts of ways that foundation assets could be used or abused." And when the Secretary was further asked, "Would you agree that many foundations have unlimited powers to buy, sell, and speculate in stocks, just as if they were private investment corporations of boundless powers with no public duties or responsibilities, and not dependent on public confidence?" he again agreed, saying, "I think they generally have unlimited powers to buy and sell, and that would presumably give them the powers to speculate if they so desire. . . ."

By their very structure, foundations easily lend themselves to a kind of righteous hocus-pocus. During the four years 1961 through 1964, the Standard Oil (Indiana) Foundation of Chicago made charitable grants totaling $5,459,967. Of this benevolence, $2,059,736, or almost thirty-eight per cent, was lateraled to the American Oil Foundation of Chicago, which is controlled by Standard Oil Company of Indiana.

The older foundations, as a rule, know how to perform their legerdemain with a degree of decorum, but not always; some of the newer foundations slip into a form of low comedy. Thus, we find the congenial Internal Revenue Service granting tax-exempt status on July 6, 1964, to the Playboy Foundation of Chicago, Illinois, which, according to the *Washington Star*, contemplates using part of its tax-free funds for "a study of the effect of smut on public morals."

Meanwhile, in Oregon, such things were being done through the St. Genevieve Foundation as to give substance to the statement made by former internal Revenue Commissioner Mortimer Caplin: "There seems to be almost no limit to what the foundations can do." The creator of the St. Genevieve Foundation, Spencer R. Collins, a millionaire in his late sixties, supported twin sisters through several years of parties and gay living, spending an estimated $100,000 on them; part of the expenses were paid by the tax-exempt foundation. One of the twins lived in a posh duplex, and spent more than $3,-000 on clothes one year. The other twin, ensconced in a five-bedroom mansion on Lake Oswego, was paid $36,000 as a "caretaker of the house," Collins admitted. This friendship was actually paid for in large measure, of course, by the U.S. taxpayer.

Collins' defense of his income tax evasion—for which he was convicted—was that he needed companionship and knew no other way to obtain it. Just how much companionship is being supported in this routine tax-exempt way is not known, since IRS keeps only the loosest check on foundations, but there is no reason to suppose that tax-exempt, high-living friendships are appealing only to the founder of an Oregon foundation and not to founders in New York, Florida, or elsewhere.

Other types of pastimes are supported by U.S. taxpayers through IRS largesse in setting up foundations for almost any purpose and then allowing them to operate more or less on the honor system. For instance, at the University of Miami in Florida there is the Julian S. Eaton Educational Foundation, whose administrators claim to have paid out $150,000 in interest-free loans to needy students. "This organization's primary function is to aid the University of Miami football team by helping recruit prospective players and making loans to needy students," as it so states in one of its mailing pieces. Once a year, boosters of the football team who have paid their $100 annual dues get together for a big blowout. Free and tax-free, of course. The U.S. Government, in effect, pays a large share of the bill.

Tax-exempt foundations could also conceivably have political uses. For example, would it not be an invaluable asset for an important politician in an important state to have some method by which he could hire a full-time liaison man—and be able to deduct that expense as a charitable item? That would be a politician's dream, and one cannot help but wonder to what extent foundations are being used for such purposes. For example:

Between 1961 and 1964, Governor Nelson A. Rockefeller provided practically all of the funds of the Government Affairs Foundation, Inc., of Albany, New York—a foundation which received $310,469 in gifts (all from Governor Rockefeller) and paid out exactly zero dollars for contributions, grants, scholarships, and other gifts. *The New York Times* of April 24, 1953, quoted Governor Rockefeller (one of the original incorporators of the foundation) as stating that the aim of the foundation, which was incorporated on April 25, 1953, would be "to improve quality and reduce quantity of government." Well, it did not do especially well in reducing the quantity of government in New York state, and, as the above expenditure notation indicates, it did not have much luck finding other worthy outlets for its money.

However, it should not be supposed that just because a foundation operates in a beneficent vacuum that it is without expenses. Quite the contrary. This Rockefeller-controlled foundation, during the four years 1961 through 1964, paid out $120,000 in salary to Frank C. Moore, former Lieutenant Governor of New York. Additionally, during the same period, Moore received $10,000 per year expense account allowance. The $160,000 paid to Moore during that period represents approximately fifty-seven per cent of the foundation's total expenses of $284,193, and about fifty-two per cent of the $310,469 contributed to the foundation by Governor Rockefeller.

The Government Affairs Foundation, Inc., made no contributions to charity or to education, but it was a busy place (rent $18,360 for four years), nonetheless, laying out $66,348 in "other salaries and wages," $1,994 for travel, $17,752 for that wonderful catch-all, "consultant fees," $1,600 for audit fees, $6,083 for telephone and telegraph, $1,708 for "books and publications," $6,385 for "general expense," $1,360 for "printing and mailing," and so on.

Big business and its offspring, the tax-exempt foundation, seem much more concerned about what the Government does with its money than about how they spend their own. Thus, not many months ago, the Morgan Guaranty Trust Company of New York, one of the nation's largest banks, issued a report warning of "the welfare wave of the future" and of "a point beyond which society cannot transfer purchasing power from its productive members to those who do not produce lest it inflict more damage than it cures." In short, Morgan Guaranty thinks the Federal Government does too much do-gooding.

One might logically inquire, if Morgan Guaranty feels this way why it is not more disposed to take up the slack?

Morgan Guaranty owns two foundations—Morgan Guaranty Trust Company of New York Foundation (tax exemption granted in 1954) and Morgan Guaranty Trust Company of New York Charitable Trust (tax exemption granted in 1962). One might inquire why the Morgan Guaranty Trust Company of New York Foundation paid out only $2.2 million in grants and gifts during the eleven years 1954 through 1964 although it had total receipts of $2.9 million. One might also inquire why the Morgan Guaranty Trust Company of New York Charitable Trust paid out only $545,399 during the three-year period 1962 through 1964, although its receipts totaled $1.6 million during that period.

The report of the Morgan Guaranty Trust Company complains of Federal expansion, but if there is any monetary dukedom that has led the way in invidious expansion, it is that of the foundations. The Richard King Mellon Foundation's assets were worth $1,000 in 1947 as against $121 million seventeen years later. Other remarkable expansions include the Mellon-controlled Bollingen Foundation, of New York City, up from $101,713 assets in 1945 to $5.1 million in 1964; the Ford Motor Company Foundation, up from nothing at its incorporation in 1949 to $38 million assets in 1964; the Standard Oil Foundation, Inc., of Chicago, up from zero assets in 1952 to holdings worth almost $49 million in 1964.

These swollen profits are contrary to the philosophy of some foundation founders. The late Dr. Max Mason, who headed the Rockefeller Foundation from 1929 to the early 1930's said, in an interview with a magazine writer seven years ago: "Old man Rockefeller did not set up the foundation, or any of his philanthropic enterprises for that matter, with the idea of everlastingness. Not only was the interest to be spent, the principal was too; so the prospect of spending itself out of existence had been before the Rockefeller Foundation from its beginnings." Yet today the Rockefeller Foundation is twenty-four times larger than it was in 1913.

Moreover, in 1929, Julius Rosenwald, who established the foundation that carried his name, wrote in the May issue of the *Atlantic Monthly*, "It is a noteworthy fact, though not as widely known as it should be, that the Rockefeller foundations are not perpetuities. If any of them today are wealthier than at their establishment, it is not because the trustees are not free to spend principal when the occasion rises."

The Rockefeller Foundation today broods over a nest egg of more than $860 million compared with $35.9 million in 1913. As for Rosenwald's philosophy, he said, "I am opposed to gifts in perpetuity for any purpose." And the next year he stated his position even more firmly: "For many years I have been convinced that it is wasteful to tie up money in perpetual trusts and that these trusts are often actually harmful in their influence."

Rosenwald's observation, though thirty-eight years old, is as appropriate today as it was then. It is clear that numerous foundations violate the spirit of their charters by hoarding rather than giving; they also violate the principle of the era upon which their founders established them. . . .

The Subcommittee can point to some notable successes. Four voluminous studies, coupled with a report of several days' hearings—a total of 1,500 pages—have been issued by this Subcommittee. Facts uncovered by the Subcommittee have stirred the Treasury into a flurry of activity with the result that seven of the 575 foundations under study have been assessed $28 million in taxes by the Treasury.

There is the beginning of a decay of public confidence in the touted integrity of foundations. For this the foundations must share a large part of the blame. Since many of the foundations show little or no disposition to police themselves, the most effective and speedy way to reform them—in the public interest—is to pass remedial Federal tax legislation and enforce it diligently.

TAXING THE FOUNDATIONS *

It's A widespread illusion that the $20.5 billion in assets held by foundations represents a possible windfall for tax relief. It doesn't.

* "Taxing the Foundations," an editorial from the *Christian Science Monitor*, March 8, 1969.

If foundations were taxed 20 percent on their $1.5 billion yearly investment income, as certain congressmen have proposed, the yield would be $300 million. If they also paid a 20 percent tax on capital gains, they would perhaps give the public coffers another $200 million. Yet this total is less than half of 1 percent of the $128 billion paid in individual and corporate taxes in the last fiscal year.

Furthermore, it is unlikely that Congress will pass the legislation to exact such a tax. It shouldn't. Foundations through their grants, provide the seed money for programs in education, the arts and sciences, and social welfare for which there would be no other support. These have an eventual impact far greater than the value of the dollars invested. Awkward or controversial grants, such as those of the Ford Foundation to former Kennedy men are the exception, and should not be an excuse for punishment.

To tax foundations would also raise the question of taxing other tax-exempt institutions, also committed to the public interest. Foundations receive about 10 percent of the $15.6 billion in voluntary gifts each year, while churches get almost half (and engage in many activities closed to foundations). Universities and private social welfare groups also receive large sums tax-free and have vast holdings, but it would be shortsighted to reduce their effectiveness by taxing them.

The real issue with foundations today is regulation. The consensus of responsible foundation leaders who testified before Congress recently was favorable to the Treasury proposals of 1965. These proposals would end various forms of self-dealing and tax evasion and the use of foundations to perpetuate family control of a business.

The Treasury isn't equipped to police grants and decisions of the foundations. What is most needed, along with basic legislated reforms, is complete disclosure of foundation finances and activities, and a uniform code of ethics.

The overseeing of foundations' activities should remain with their trustees and the attorneys general of the chartering states. It would be a pity to hamper the freedom of decision which, more than their money, makes private foundations so valuable a counterbalance to the good-doing agencies of the government.

REMARKS BEFORE THE HOUSE COMMITTEE ON WAYS AND MEANS *

by George Meany

MY NAME is George Meany and I am president of the American Federation of Labor and Congress of Industrial Organizations.

The 13.5 million members of the unions of the AFL-CIO are, almost without exception, taxpayers. They pay their taxes regularly, payday after payday, through the payroll withholding program. They are loyal Americans; they appreciate the value of government, the services of government, the need for paying for government.

They are willing to pay their fair share.

But they are tired, Mr. Chairman, of having to pay the

* These remarks were made before the Committee on Ways and Means of the House of Representatives, April 1, 1969. They were inserted into the *Congressional Record* on April 14, 1969 by Hon. Lee Metcalf of Montana. George Meany has been president of the American Federation of Labor since 1952 and of the AFL-CIO since 1955.

share of other Americans. They are specifically tired of paying the share of those Americans whose incomes are greater and whose taxes are lower—the "loophole set" in today's society.

So it is on behalf of the largest organized group of taxpayers in America, Mr. Chairman, that we come here today with proposals we believe are based on the doctrine of fair play. There are some who call the measures before this Committee "tax reform." We think "tax justice" is a better description and that is what we are seeking here today—tax justice.

The federal income-tax structure has drifted far afield from the American standard of fair play. It is rigged against income from work and against wage and salary earners. It is rigged in favor of unearned income. Because of these facts, confidence in our tax system has eroded. This erosion must be ended. Fairness in federal taxation must be restored.

In our appendix statement we have catalogued what we believe to be the most glaring abuses—the loopholes and gimmicks which lighten the tax burdens of those who have both huge amounts of unearned income and great ability to pay and yet who unfairly rig the nation's tax structure against those whose livelihood depends on a paycheck.

This program of tax justice we urge is ambitious and far-reaching, long overdue and critically urgent. There is no longer time for pause, delay, gestures or tokens. . . .

The tax-exempt status granted to certain foundations represents one of the most glaring examples of how a well-intentioned, seemingly desirable, tax privilege can become twisted.

As a nation, we recognize that philanthropy is desirable and it should be encouraged. In line with this reasoning, individuals are permitted, within certain limits, to deduct from their taxable income, contributions to organizations established for

religious, charitable, scientific, educational and similar purposes. Likewise, the federal government grants tax-exempt
status to the organizations receiving the contributions.

Granting special tax privileges for such contributions or to
such institutions raises the same fundamental question as in all
tax-forgiveness schemes. The government is relinquishing
funds it would otherwise be entitled to, and therefore others
must pay a higher share of the costs of government. Thus,
where there is tax forgiveness, there must also be an assurance
that the nation's interests are being served.

Recent investigations into certain tax-exempt foundations
—non-profit organizations set up and supported by wealthy
families or individuals—have raised some serious doubts as to
whether appropriate purposes are in fact being fulfilled and
the nation's interest is being served.

Tax-exempt foundations have grown phenomenally—new
ones are cropping up at the rate of some 2,000 per year. The
assets of the larger foundations are currently estimated at
some $20 billion, and each of the 27 largest foundations has as-
sets worth $100 million or more.

The philosophy underlying the private foundations, according to a foundation spokesman is "the systematic use of private funds for public purposes." Unfortunately, the studies of
the activities of tax-exempt foundations done by the House
Committee on Small Business have shown that in many cases
the opposite situation prevails. That is, public funds are being
systematically used for private purposes.

Family foundations frequently are used as a means whereby
the wealthy can avoid income, gift and inheritance taxes, yet
maintain control over wealth. When families donate company
stock to private family-run foundations, family control over
the business can be assured from generation to generation,
while inheritance taxes are avoided. The donor can control

the management of the foundation—appointing relatives, rewarding friends and employees. The foundation provides the conduit for donations which reduce the taxes on his business income.

Furthermore, this control can be parlayed to a point where the foundation is used to promote the foundation owner's other business interests. Practices have been uncovered which can be questioned on the basis of unfair competition, conflict of interest, self-dealing, "insider" arrangements to affect stock prices, and so forth.

Foundations, for example, can lend money to the founder, his family, or the family business at preferential interest rates, thus supplying venture capital for the donor's other interests. The Subcommittee's studies noted situations, where suppliers and buyers have made sizable contributions to foundations, controlled by customers, indicating underhanded pricing deals. What's more, these organizations can enter into deals, whereby through intricate tax maneuvering, they can buy a business, invest none of their own money, and pay the seller more than the market value of the business. On top of this, the deal can be set up as an installment purchase, permitting the seller to convert what should have been ordinary income into preferentially taxed capital gains.

A Prentice-Hall Executive Tax Report, for example, offers this advice:

"Have You Put a Price on Your Business? You may be able to double it—by selling to a Charity.

"Say you're planning to sell your business and you think a fair price would be five times earnings. If the company earns, say, $101,500 after taxes ($200,000 before), you're probably figuring on selling for about $500,000. If that's the case, stop right there—you may be shortchanging yourself:

"That business could be worth $1,000,000 to a tax-exempt organization: An ordinary buyer is only interested in earnings after taxes—that's all he gets to see. But a tax-exempt buyer keeps a hundred cents on the dollar. So a fair price to a charity would be five times $200,000, or $1,000,000—twice what you figured!"

Finally, the Report notes some "Frosting on the cake" and cites a case where the seller maintained 48% ownership of the corporation, "was active in management and drew a good salary."

Commenting on the abuses uncovered, a *New York Times* editorial added another dimension—that of the increased role of foundations in shaping national policy:

"Since almost everyone pays income taxes, the burden of exempting the income of the foundations is borne by the public at large. Yet the public is virtually powerless to influence the ways in which the foundations spend their tax-free dollars."

Generous tax treatment is appropriate for charitable organizations since private philanthropy is an important adjunct to public programs serving the goals of the nation. However, this special treatment is justifiable only if these organizations are in fact using the foundations, and their tax-exempt privilege, for the public good and not merely for the private advantage of a select well-heeled few. . . .

[Proposals]

Tax-Exempt Foundations: (1) Financial transactions between a foundation and its founders, contributors, officers, directors or trustees should be prohibited.

(2) Foundations should be required to spend their incomes within one year of receipt.

(3) Foundations should not be permitted to own 20% or

more of any business unrelated to their charitable function—a reasonable time should be allowed for presently organized foundations to comply with this provision.

(4) If a donor maintains control of a business or property after it is contributed, no donation deduction from taxes should be allowed until the foundation disposes of the property or the donor's control over the property ends.

(5) Foundation borrowing to buy investment properties should be prohibited. Foundation lending should be limited to appropriate charitable functions.

(6) A limitation, such as 40 years, should be placed on the life of foundations.

(7) Congress should carefully examine the problems posed by the actual operations of foundations and the need for some degree of federal regulation of the use of the tax-exempt funds of foundations.

TAXING FOUNDATIONS
IS DANGEROUS *

by John W. Gardner

It is said that the best time to repent of a blunder is just before the blunder is made. The House Ways and Means Committee and Congress have a rare opportunity for such fore-

* "A Whip That Could Cripple Many Public Services," Washington *Post*, June 8, 1969. John W. Gardner headed the Carnegie Corporation of New York for ten years and was Secretary of Health, Education, and Welfare in the Johnson Administration. In 1968 he became chairman of the Urban Coalition, an organization which depends in part upon foundation grants.

sightedness. It is to be found in the committee's highly controversial "tentative proposals" for dealing with the tax exemption of foundations.

The committee's proposals include a number of excellent measures designed to correct abuses. In some cases, donors have established foundations as tax havens and have shamelessly manipulated foundation funds for their personal benefit rather than for the public good.

Leaders in the foundation field have long advocated the correction of such abuses. The new corrective measures, plus more aggressive enforcement, will help enormously. The wicked flee when no man pursueth, but as someone pointed out, they make better time when the righteous are after them.

But in the Ways and Means Committee's tentative proposals are other items that have created widespread astonishment and consternation among tax-exempt organizations, not only foundations but all other research and educational organizations in the private sector. . . .

Finally, the tentative proposals recommend that a 5 per cent tax on net investment income be levied against foundations (and against all the tax-exempt organizations included in the new, broadened definition). Though 5 per cent seems like a modest assessment, leaders in the private sector are deeply concerned that it may be the beginning of the end of tax exemption for charitable, educational and scientific activities in this country.

It is worth remembering that tax exemption is a means of preserving the strength of the private sector and insuring that our cultural and educational life is not wholly subject to the monolithic dictates of government. It would be quite possible for a nation to insist that government be the sole source of support for all educational, scientific, charitable and perhaps even religious activities—and in some nations, the government is precisely that. But our policy of tax exemption asserts that it is in the public interest for many varied groups outside of government to be engaged in charitable, religious and educational activities.

The policy is based on the wise conviction that we will be better off if these activities so crucial to the core of our national life are participated in by individuals and groups with a wide range of points of view. We don't believe that Big Government has all the answers; we want a lot of people in the act.

In the light of history, it is an audacious doctrine. Most human societies have not tolerated religious institutions other than the official established religion. We not only tolerate them; we say that it is in the public interest to foster them through tax exemption.

We foster private schools with a great variety of educational philosophies, universities in which every kind of idea is freely discussed, scientific institutions that are free to go where their intellectual curiosity takes them. In short, tax exemption is one of the devices by which our free society has encouraged diversity and innovation.

It would be strange indeed if those with totalitarian tendencies had not chafed under such practices, and of course they have. Perhaps the most dramatic and explicit attack came from the late Sen. Joseph McCarthy, who was outraged because some foundation money had gone to activities he thought ill of. He asserted that the foundations were using money that, but for tax exemption, would go into the Federal Treasury and that therefore Congress had a right to examine the ideas and activities supported by the foundations to determine their acceptability.

He was setting forth a radical doctrine. Applied with logical consistency, it would have given the Federal Government absolute right of review over the ideas and philosophies of every school, university and church in the Nation. It would have ended experimentation and established a Federally supervised orthodoxy.

The proponents of the tax say, "It's only 5 per cent—surely little enough." But if Congress, in a fit of annoyance at the foundations, can levy a 5 per cent tax this year, it can double it the next time it is annoyed at the foundations. Depending on its level of annoyance, it can tax them 25 per cent or 100 per cent.

And, of course, foundations aren't the only nonprofit organizations that can be annoying. The universities are currently the subject of considerable public opprobrium. Will they be next? At times in the past, one or another church has been unpopular with the majority of the populace. How soon will they be hit? There is nothing in the logic of the tax on foundations that cannot be applied with equal cogency to all tax-exempt organizations.

If a tax is levied, the impact will be felt among all kinds of tax-exempt organizations. The money used to pay the tax would have been paid out by the foundations in grants to universities, hospitals, churches, cancer clinics, scholarship programs and so on. When the tax is levied, those potential recipients will bear the loss. And to the extent that this diminishes private sector sources of support, it makes those recipients turn more insistently to Federal support. Where is the wisdom of that?

The gain in tax receipts—an estimated $65 million to $75 million—would be a negligible fraction of Federal revenues. And that gain could be wiped out by costs of collection and enforcement plus the likelihood that the Government would have to make up at least part of the loss to institutions dependent on foundation support.

An uninformed observer might suppose that organizations subject to such discriminatory treatment must have behaved very badly indeed. But a review of the record reveals no such thing. On the contrary, the leading foundations have been among the most reputable and distinguished organizations in our national life.

They have achieved that distinction with an annual income that is tiny compared to national expenditures in cultural, educational and scientific fields. And they operate under more unsparing public scrutiny than is visited upon almost any other organization in our national life.

Selected Bibliography
and Index

Selected Bibliography

Andrews, F. Emerson. *Attitudes Toward Giving*. New York: Russell Sage Foundation, 1953. Personal interviews stressing the higher motives behind foundations.

———. *Philanthropic Foundations*. New York: Russell Sage Foundation, 1956. Still the best single survey of foundations, though, of course, out of date.

———. "Philanthropy's Venture Capital." *Education Record*, 32 (October, 1951), 361–370. Important for comparison with current possibilities for foundation innovation.

———, ed. *Foundations—20 Viewpoints*. New York: Russell Sage Foundation, 1965. Evaluations of current foundation programs and problems from friendly sources.

Belknap, Chauncey, and Philip Mandel. *The Federal Income Tax Exemption of Charitable Organizations: Its History and Underlying Policy*. New York: Patterson, Belknap, and Webb, 1954. Strong on foundation theory.

Bremner, Robert H. *American Philanthropy*. Chicago: University of Chicago Press, 1969. A first-rate survey, learned and provocative.

Burnham, James. "Sock It to Us, Herbert: Foundation Money for New Left Teaching." *National Review*, 20 (November 19, 1968), 1158.

Clark, Elias. "The Limitation on Political Activities: A Discordant Note in the Law of Charities." *Virginia Law Review*, 46 (April, 1960), 439–466.

Coffman, Harold C. *American Foundations: A Study of Their Role in the Child Welfare Movement.* New York: Association Press, 1936. An early critical survey with valuable statistical information.

Coon, Horace. *Money to Burn: What the Great American Philanthropic Foundations Do with Their Money.* New York: Longmans, Green, 1938. A popular treatment raising important questions.

Cousins, Norman. "New Directions for American Foundations." *Saturday Review,* 35 (September 13, 1952), 24.

Eaton, Berrien C., Jr. "Charitable Foundations and Related Matters under the 1950 Revenue Act." *Virginia Law Review,* 37 (January, 1951), 1–54; (February, 1951), 253–296. The best source for understanding the "fiendishly complicated" Revenue Act of 1950.

Eells, Richard. *The Corporation and the Arts.* New York: Macmillan, 1967. A convincing case for the philanthropic support of the arts.

Embree, Edwin R. "Timid Billions: Are the Foundations Doing Their Job?" *Harper's Magazine,* 198 (March, 1949), 28–37. An early challenge to foundation "venture capital."

Flexner, Abraham, with Esther S. Bailey. *Funds and Foundations: Their Policies, Past and Present.* New York: Harper, 1952. An experienced educator and philanthropoid criticizes modern foundation activities.

Ford Foundation. *Report of the Study for the Ford Foundation on Policy and Program.* Detroit: Ford Foundation, 1949. An exhaustive statement of philanthropic principles created for the guidance of the nation's wealthiest foundation. To be compared with a similar document published in 1962 by the Foundation setting goals for the next decade.

Fosdick, Raymond B. *A Philosophy for a Foundation, on the Fiftieth Anniversary of the Rockefeller Foundation, 1913–1963.* New York: Rockefeller Foundation, 1963.

Foundation News. The bulletin of The Foundation Center, published bimonthly since 1960. An invaluable source of information and partisan opinion.

Fremont-Smith, Marion R. *Foundations and Government: State and Federal Law and Supervision.* New York: Russell Sage Foundation, 1965. A rewarding study of foundations as legal instrumentalities, marred by polemics against foundation critics.

Fulton, William. "Let's Look at Our Foundations." *American Legion Magazine,* 52 (August, 1952), 22–23, 42–44. Predictable condemnations of foundations from the McCarthy Era.

Gardner, John W. "Foundation Operating Policies." *Association of American Colleges Bulletin,* 42 (March, 1956), 78–85. A set of guiding principles by the President of the Carnegie Corporation.

Karst, Kenneth L. "The Tax Exemption of Donor-Controlled Foundations." *Ohio State Law Journal,* 25, (1964), 188–221.

Kelle, Harold M. "Government's Attitude toward Foundations." *Michigan State Bar Journal,* 33 (October, 1954), 9–25. An interesting paper on smaller foundations and critics.

Keppel, Frederick P. *The Foundation: Its Place in American Life* New York: Macmillan, 1930. An overly-general but humane vision of the philanthropic possibilities awaiting foundations, as seen from the Depression.

Kiger, Joseph C. *Operating Principles of the Larger Foundations.* New York: Russell Sage Foundation, 1954. A biased but useful survey of data collected by the Cox Committee.

Kirstein, G. G. "Philanthropy: The Golden Crowbar." *The Nation,* 207 (September 16, 1968), 235–240. A dour look at foundations as tax advantages.

Lankford, John. *Congress and the Foundations in the Twentieth Century.* River Falls, Wisconsin: Wisconsin State University, 1964. A brief study of the Walsh, Cox, Reece, and Patman investigations.

Lasser, J. K. "Why Do So Many Business Men Start Foundations?" *Dun's Review,* 57 (February, 1949), 15–17, 35–44. A frank discussion of the business advantages offered by foundations.

Lewis, Marianna O. ed. *Foundation Directory, Edition III.* New York: Russell Sage Foundation, 1967. Data on 6,803 foundations.

Macdonald, Dwight. *The Ford Foundation: The Men and the Millions.* New York: Reynal, 1956. A light-handed, witty survey of the Ford Foundation, written originally as a series of articles in the *New Yorker.*

Marts, Arnaud C. *The Generosity of Americans.* Englewood Cliffs, New Jersey: Prentice-Hall, 1966. Data on American giving.

Miller, H. H. "Investigating the Foundations." *Reporter,* 9 (November 24, 1953), 37–40. On the political origins of the Cox and Reece Committee investigations.

Neilsen, Waldemar A. "How Solid Are the Foundations?" New York *Times* Magazine, October 21, 1962, p. 27. A former Ford Foundation official assigns the temerity of the larger foundations to the Cox and Reece investigations.

Nelson, Ralph L. *The Investment Policies of Foundations.* New York: Russell Sage Foundation, 1967.

Reeves, Thomas C. "Foundations in Blinders: The Cool Billions." *The Nation,* 202 (April 4, 1966), 381–385.

——. *Freedom and the Foundation: The Fund for the Republic in the Era of McCarthyism.* New York: Alfred A. Knopf, 1969.

——. "The Foundation and Freedoms: An Inquiry into the Origins of the Fund for the Republic," *Pacific Historical Review,* 34 (1965), 197–218.

Report of the Princeton Conference on the History of Philanthropy in the United States. New York: Russell Sage Foundation, 1956. Contains an extensive annotated bibliography on American philanthropy.

Riecker, John E. "Foundations and the Patman Committee Report." *Michigan Law Review,* 63 (November 1964), 95–140. Critical and suggestive.

Slichter, Sumner H. "Undermining the Foundations." *Atlantic Monthly,* 194 (September, 1954), 50–54. An intelligent assault upon the Reece Committee.

Stern, Philip. *The Great Treasury Raid.* New York: Random House, 1964. Still the classic work on tax avoidance.

Sugerman, Norman A., and Harlan Pomeroy. "Business Income of Exempt Organizations." *Virginia Law Review,* 46 (April, 1960), 424–438.

Taft, J. Richard. *Understanding Foundations: Dimensions in Fund Raising.* New York: McGraw-Hill, 1967. An excellent analysis of current foundation problems and opportunities, containing a useful guide to a select number of foundations.

Tax-Exempt Foundations and Charitable Trusts: Their Impact on Our Economy (Second Installment). Subcommittee Chairman's Report to Subcommittee No. 1, Select Committee on Small Business, House of Representatives, 88th Cong., 1st Sess. Washington, D.C.: Government Printing Office, October 16, 1963. Congressman Patman's second report.

Tax-Exempt Foundations and Charitable Trusts: Their Impact on Our Economy (Third Installment). Subcommittee Chairman's Report to Subcommittee No. 1, Select Committee on Small Business, House of Representatives, 88th Cong. Washington, D.C.: Government Printing Office, March 20, 1964. The third report, an analysis of the Alfred I. du Pont Estate and its affiliate, the Nemours Foundation.

Tax-Exempt Foundations: Their Impact on Small Business. Hearings before Subcommittee No. 1 on Foundations, Select Committee on Small Business, House of Representatives, 88th Cong., 2d Sess. Washington, D.C.: Government Printing Office, 1964. Patman confronting Treasury officials.

Tax-Exempt Foundations and Charitable Trusts: Their Impact on Our Economy (Fifth Installment). Subcommittee Chairman's Report to Subcommittee No. 1, Select Committee on Small Business, House of Representatives, 90th Cong. Washington, D.C.: Government Printing Office, April 28, 1967. Over 1,100 pages of exhibits relating to the James Irvine Foundation-Irvine Company, of Orange County, California.

Tax-Exempt Foundations and Charitable Trusts: Their Impact on Our Economy (Sixth Installment). Subcommittee Chairman's Report to Subcommittee No. 1, Select Committee on Small Business, House of Representatives, 90th Cong. Washington, D.C.: Government Printing Office, March 26, 1968. Largely a general survey of the financial statistics of 596 foundations from 1965 through 1966, including a request "that for the duration of the Vietnam war the tax-exempt foundations and charitable trusts of this country contribute their gross receipts . . . to the Federal Government in support of our defense of democracy in Southeast Asia and other uses vital to our national interest."

Traylor, Eleanor K. *Public Accountability of Foundations and Charitable Trusts.* New York: Russell Sage Foundation, 1953.

U.S., House of Representatives. *Hearings Before the Select (Cox) Committee to Investigate Tax-Exempt Foundations and Comparable Organizations.* 82d Cong., 2d Sess. Washington, D.C.: Government Printing Office, 1953. 792 pages of testimony, often valuable.

———. *Final Report of the Select (Cox) Committee to Investigate Foundations and Other Organizations.* 82d Cong., 2d Sess. House Report No. 2514. Washington, D.C.: Government Printing Office, 1953. The 15-page conclusions of the Committee.

———. *Hearings Before the Special (Reece) Committee to Investigate Tax-Exempt Foundations and Comparable Organizations.* Part 1. 83d Cong., 2d Sess. Washington, D.C.: Government Printing Office, 1954. Lengthy testimony by Committee witnesses.

——. *Hearings.* Part II. 83d Cong., 2d Sess. Washington: Government Printing Office, 1954, pp. 945–1241. Written replies from several foundations to Committee charges, plus additional Committee materials.

——. *Tax-Exempt Foundations: Report of the Special Committee to Investigate Tax-Exempt Foundations and Comparable Organizations.* 83d Cong., 2d Sess. House Report No. 2681. Washington, D.C.: Government Printing Office, 1954. Contains the majority and minority reports, as well as an index to both the Reece and Cox hearings.

Varney, Harold Lord. "Are the Foundations Untouchable?" *American Legion Magazine,* 58 (June, 1955), 18–19, 54–59. A view from the Far Right.

Weithorn, Stanley S. *Tax Techniques for Foundations and Other Exempt Organizations.* New York: Matthew Bender, 1964.

"Why Business Is Finding More Use for Foundations." *Business Week,* June 19, 1954, pp. 166–178.

"Why the Foundations Are under Fire." *U.S. News and World Report,* 54 (January 21, 1963), 83–85.

Whyte, William H., Jr. "What Are the Foundations up to?" *Fortune,* 52 (October, 1955), 110–113, 254–260.

——. "Where the Foundations Fall Down." *Fortune,* 52 (November, 1955), 140–141, 211–220. Critical examinations of shortcomings of the Ford, Rockefeller, and Carnegie foundations.

Yarmolinsky, Adam. "How to Run a Small Foundation." *Harper's Magazine,* 222 (April, 1961), 80–84.

Index

Albert, C. B., 107
American Association for the Advancement of Science, 111
American Association for the United Nations, 109, 112
American Association of International Conciliation, 111
American Bar Association, 21
American Box Board Company Foundation, 200
American Council of Christian Churches, 122
American Council of Independent Laboratories, 166
American Council of Learned Societies, 102, 111
American Council on Education, 111
American Dilemma, An, 93
American Economic Foundation, 122–124, 126
American Enterprise Association, 126
American Enterprise Institute for Public Policy Research, 126, 131
American Federation of Labor, 209
American Federation of State, County, and Municipal Employees, 145
American Foundation for Political Education, 109
American Foundations: A Study of Their Role in the Child Welfare Movement, 9
American Friends of the Middle East, 133–135, 139–141, 145

American Friends Service Committee, 115
American Future, Inc., 122
American Historical Association, 111
American International Association for Economic and Social Development, 170
American Labor Education Service, 109
American Legion, 135
American Library Association, 109
American Newspaper Guild, 145
American Oil Foundation, 202
American Opinion, 139
American Peace Society, 112
American Philosophical Society, 90
American Political Science Association, 101
Americans for the Competitive Enterprise System, 126
Americans for Constitutional Actions, 129
Andrews, F. Emerson, 3, 4, 9, 13, 49, 185
Andrews, Glen, 135
Anti-Defamation League (B'nai B'rith), 120
Arensberg, Mariada C., 136–139
Armstrong, George W., Jr., 130
Association of Hungarian Students in North America, 145
Atlantic Acceptance Corporation of Canada, 199
Atlantic Monthly, 206
Avalon Foundation, 170